D0470728

## PRAISE FOR *JESUS NEVER SAID TO PLANT CHURCHES*

"This is a go-to guide for those thinking about the adventure of a church plant. Trinity has written a super helpful tool to challenge and discover our true calling. A must read for every current or future planter."

—Mike Foster
Founder of PlainJoe Studios and
People of the Second Chance

"Trinity Jordan addresses the core principles that must guide every church planter. Don't plant a church without reading this book."

—Steve Pike
National director of Church Multiplication Network

"If you're thinking about planting a church, you've got to read this book. It's a gold mine. Trinity is talking about stuff I don't hear a lot of church planters talk about. He's honest and inspiring. I love this guy. Trinity is the real deal."

—Scott Wilson
Senior pastor of The Oaks Fellowship and author of *Act Normal*

"Trinity takes a fun, witty, and at times sarcastic look at what it truly takes to plant churches and do ministry in a next-generation context. His mix of the practical with real stories and authentic emotion is the perfect combination. Trinity Jordan gets it right, big time!"

—Matthew Keller
Lead pastor of Next Level Church (Ft. Myers, FL)
and founder of Next Level Coaching

"The message of this book may be offensive to some and comforting to others. I'm glad someone finally chose to be vulnerable enough to share the good, bad, and the ugly about church planting."

—Bryan Jarett
Lead pastor of Northplace Church (Sachse, TX)

"Trinity's church planting experience in the Salt Lake Valley offers a twenty-first century example of what is possible when we obey Christ's command to make disciples; it results in a vibrant community of people whose life together actually draws broken people toward the transforming power of the gospel. That process is simpler than you think yet harder than you could ever imagine."

—Byron Klaus
President of Assemblies of God Theological Seminary

"Reading this book might talk you out of planting a church, but it also may save your life! This is valuable insight from someone who has walked the trail before you!"

—Rob Ketterling
Lead pastor of River Valley Church (Apple Valley, MN)
and lead team member of ARC

"I am a huge fan of guys like Trinity, who have the guts to not only pursue the calling of being architects of *ekklesia* and community, but who actually live to tell about it! I guarantee that every kingdom entrepreneur I've been blessed to serve around the world would have loved to have this as part of their survival kit 'back in the day.'"

—Mel McGowan
President and founder of Visioneering Studios

"Church planting is close to the heart of God. Church planter Trinity Jordan rightly recognizes that church planting without discipleship is a misguided endeavor. Church planters must elevate the work of discipleship as the highest priority in their ministry."

—Ed Stetzer

www.edstetzer.com and

coauthor of *Viral Churches*


"Based on his own experience, Trinity Jordan tells prospective church planters all the things they wish they had known *before* they started. This volume is a boot camp in a book."

—Earl Creps

Associate professor and director of D.Min. program at

Assemblies of God Theological Seminary

and author of *Reverse Mentoring*


"Aside from being funny, you'll find Trinity to be like a blunt and honest friend—the kind who will spare you a few church heartaches while making you laugh. Get ready for a fresh spin on church planting."

—Peter Haas

Lead pastor of Substance Church (Roseville, MN)

and author of *Pharisectomy*

AS

Brother it was great meeting with you & your wife. You are amazing! Keep in touch! And go make those disciples.

Gal 2:20

trinityjordan@gmail.com

# JESUS NEVER SAID TO PLANT CHURCHES

# JESUS NEVER SAID TO PLANT CHURCHES

AND 12 MORE THINGS THEY NEVER
TOLD ME ABOUT CHURCH PLANTING

## TRINITY JORDAN

 Influence

www.InfluencesResources.com
Copyright © 2012 Trinity Jordan
ALL RIGHTS RESERVED

Published by Influence Resources
1445 N. Boonville Ave., Springfield, Missouri 65802

Published in association with The Quadrivium Group—Orlando, FL
info@TheQuadriviumGroup.com

Developmental Editing by
Ben Stroup, BenStroup.com—Greenbrier, TN
Copy Editing and Proofreading by
Kyle Olund, KLO Publishing—Hendersonville, TN
Cover and Interior Design by
Lauren Murrell, Volacious—Hendersonville, TN
Cover Fonts by Riley Cran and Mike Fortress, LostType.com

No part of this book may be reproduced, stored in a retrieval system,
or transmitted in any form or by any means—electronic, mechanical,
photocopy, recording, or otherwise—without prior written permission
of the copyright owner, except brief quotations used in connection with
reviews in magazines or newspapers.

Scripture quotations are from The Holy Bible, English Standard Version®
(ESV®), copyright © 2001 by Crossway, a publishing ministry of Good News
Publishers. Used by permission. All rights reserved.

ISBN: 978-1-93669-981-0
First printing 2012
Printed in United States of America

*This book is dedicated first and foremost
to my Lord, Messiah Jesus.
I try to live as You have taught
and I try to follow You in all I do.*

*Also, to my wife, Ami, my best friend and love of my life.*

*And to my daddy's girls, Madison and Berlyn.*

*To the team that gave everything to plant a church with me,
Ryan & Molly Lind, Brandon Irwin, Shelby Atkins, and Brendan Perko.*

*And to the churches, friends, family, and pastors who
supported us to plant churches in Utah.*

*To the people of Elevation Church.*

*And to every person who has ever felt God
urging them to plant a church.*

*This book is for you.*

# CONTENTS

# ACKNOWLEDGMENTS

I have no cape on my shoulders. I did nothing on my own. I want to extend my deepest love, respect, and gratitude to those who made this book possible.

Steve & Cheri Pike: Thank you for saying yes to God and going to Utah. Ami and I are products of your obedience to God. You will always be our parents in the faith.

Doyle Robinson and Jim Ladd: You both have served well as elders and mentors of mine as I have walked this road of church planting. I learned so much from both of you. You inspired much of the content in this book.

Ryan Lind: What do you get when God and a crazy desert camp in the mountains of Colorado are mixed with two rebellious twenty-something youth pastors? I was honored to plant Elevation Church with you and serve alongside you. I am so thankful to God that the journey was with you. You taught me more than any book or college class about how to love people at their worst.

John Jay Wilson and Steve & Susan Blount: Thank you for believing that I had a voice to share with other church planters and church leaders. I am humbled to be part of Influence Resources.

To Elevation Church staff, leaders, and members: The generosity of grace and mercy that you have extended to me has inspired me beyond what you will ever understand. Thank you for allowing me so much leeway to travel, write, and experiment. I am so proud of how God is growing you as followers of Him. Your humility is inspiring, your sincerity is contagious, and your creativity is God given.

And thanks to Ami: Thank you for thinking that I did have a cape on my shoulders and believing I was your superhero. Looking into your blue eyes always makes me feel as if I could fly. I love you to the moon and back.

# Foreword

## by Mark Batterson

There are a lot of people who talk and write about church planting. It certainly is a popular topic of conversation among ministry leaders these days. As a church planter, I find it very difficult to read, listen, and learn from someone who has never done it. This is not the case with Trinity Jordan. This book was written with blood, sweat, and tears.

I've known Trinity long enough to know that he is the real thing. He is a church planter not because he has read a lot of books, attended a lot of seminars and conferences, or because he has advanced degrees in the discipline. He is a church planter not because he wears torn jeans, sips coffee at Starbucks, or uses Apple products exclusively. He is a church planter because he has done it.

When God called Trinity to plant a church, he didn't go where he would find the easiest soil to plow or the quickest harvest. God led him to Utah. I've watched Trinity grow Elevation Church from a few people to thousands who gather regularly to worship God, serve the community, and reach the lost. In fact, I've had the privilege of preaching at Elevation, so I've seen what God has done firsthand. And it's definitely a God thing.

There are a lot of misconceptions about what planting a church is all about. Too many people with good intentions set out to plant a church only to discover that it wasn't what they thought it would be.

It takes longer than you might think. It costs more money than you first budget. And the stakes are much higher emotionally, relationally, and spiritually than you first anticipate.

In spite of the cost, planting churches has proven to be a very effective way to reach the lost. It is our job to carry forth the Great Commission until Christ's return. Not everyone is called to plant a church. But if you are called, and brave enough to answer that call, then this book is for you. I wish I had read this book long ago. So much of church planting—at least the way it was presented to me early in my ministry—left me with very romantic, idealistic expectations of what my experience would be like. I learned quickly that I was underprepared and had to learn the hard way the lessons Trinity writes about.

This book is not a how-to guide to planting churches. There are plenty of those available. What's different about this book is that it will test the resolve of those feeling called to plant a church, enlighten those in the midst of the work, and expose those who never get to see this side of ministry with the pain, agony, and joy of the process. Seeing God move in and through ordinary people to accomplish things beyond our wildest imagination is what this great adventure is all about. This is what it meant when Jesus talked about the abundant life.

May the words between the covers of this book inform and inspire you to boldly follow God's leadership in your life, wherever it may lead. Amen.

**Mark Batterson**
Lead Pastor, National Community Church
Washington, D.C.

# Jesus Never Said to Plant Churches

# CHAPTER 1

# IF YOU CAN SEE YOURSELF DOING ANYTHING OTHER THAN CHURCH PLANTING, PUT THIS BOOK DOWN AND GO DO IT NOW!

*"God has a way of speaking to the heart and spirit. A way of captivating our inner desires and drives."*

Honestly, church planting is hard.

Very hard.

No one ever told me that.

All the training I went through was from guys who proclaimed, "If I can do it, you can too." I knew that church planting was going to be easy 'cause, hey—this guy did it and he looks like Guy Smiley.

It wasn't easy at all.

I would ask the question, "WHY?" so many times. Lying in bed wondering if I had made the biggest mistake of my life. Did I do this right? Did God really call me to do this?

And that is what it always came back to.

God.

I couldn't shake the God factor.

I'm not sure why anyone would want to start a church if they were not called by God to do so. I mean, I know why they try to do it.

The perception is that church planters are the cool guys in the Christian subculture. This church planting conference I went to one time even showed a video of a Mac spoof commercial where the church planter was the Mac guy and the typical traditional pastor was the PC guy. We all know that the Mac commercials are selling us what is cool and keeping us from what isn't, so the message we are constantly communicating to our Christian leaders is that church planters are the coolest of the cool.

Or there are the people who plant a church because their home church made a bad decision and so they split. Wait, I mean plant a new church in their city to follow the vision that their church should have been on.

Really the list of "why try" can be exhaustive. Yet other than God, I don't know why you would WANT to do this.

I can think of better ways of being cool and changing a decision in your former church than almost killing yourself spiritually and emotionally.

Yep.

Killing yourself.

Totally.

**Called to Be a Church Planter**

Maybe the question then is how do you know you are called by God? Which is a good question.

The answer is probably different for everyone.

I have this friend, Steve, who back when he was in his early thirties and single would ask a series of questions to every new married couple he met:

1. How did you know that you were in love?
2. When did you know they were the one to marry?
3. What made you so sure?

He so badly didn't want to miss out on his spouse in life that he was constantly studying what to look for through everyone else's marriage. The frustrating thing for Steve was that a lot of the people gave different answers, but the most heard answer was the most frustrating answer.

"I just knew."

How do you know you are called to plant a church?

You might already have a great story of how God confirmed His call to you. I've heard some cool stories before. I heard this story about this guy eating at a McDonald's in the city he was thinking of planting a church in, a city he had never been to until that day. Out of nowhere rides up a big football player of a guy on a child's bike. The guy walks into McDonald's and looks around for this soon-to-be church planter and tells him that he is to plant a church in that city. Then he leaves.

I guess if that were you or I, we would have an answer to our question. That is, if we were called to plant a church or not.

You might have one of those confirmation stories.

I do and I don't.

What we will find is that all of our stories are different.

OR

If we would be completely honest with ourselves and we would sit quietly and answer my friend Steve's question, we would probably say,

"I just know."

God has a way of speaking to the heart and spirit. A way of captivating our inner desires and drives.

I don't think He has to talk us into church planting at all. We can't do anything else. We can't rest until we have accomplished what He has laid out in our hearts for us to do.

That unrest drives us to our calling.

When the TV is off, the music has stopped playing, the kids are in bed, the house is creaking . . . you will feel the unrest inside your soul, that calling to start a church.

We might struggle along the way with questions about assurance; that is probably what it means to be human. Who doesn't want to have the seal of authenticity?

Ami and I just knew.

No big story of how we knew. We just did. Neither one of us can recall the exact moment when we went, "Eureka! We should plant a church." It just came to us. We couldn't stop talking about Utah; we couldn't stop talking about what ministry God wanted to do in Utah; and we couldn't stop thinking about all of our friends and family members who needed to hear the message of Jesus. We knew this meant a church-plant.

No guy at a McDonald's on a bike.

We just knew.

I tried to do something else.

I took the LSAT (the test you need for law school admissions) and even applied to a few law schools.

It just didn't feel right.

For the first time publicly, I will admit that I didn't get into law school on my first try.

What, are you kidding me?
I graduated at the top of the legal studies department.
I have an amazing GPA.
I scored higher than most of the people who took the LSAT.
What?

God had other plans in my life.

Funny thing is, I remember holding the envelope of the law school I really wanted to go to and thinking there is no way they said yes. I'm supposed to plant a church.

### I Just Knew

Ami and I were both twenty-four years old when we set out to plant a church roughly fifteen miles north of Salt Lake City. We started with three families and a dog named Carson. We met in a house on Monday nights for an hour and a half. Our small Jesus community began to grow. Within ten months, forty-plus people packed our home for Wednesday night house church.

We knew it was time to start another house church. In fact, we felt like it was time to start a larger, very public, gathering. That fall we launched public meetings in a movie theater with 158 people showing up from our community that first Sunday morning.

Today, we have anywhere from nine to eleven different house churches in the Salt Lake valley, two public gathering locations, and we are working on multiplying our house churches even more as well as developing another large gathering location.

Knowing doesn't mean you don't want to be reassured along the way. For some reason, doubt will creep into your mind as you begin your journey to plant a church. It appears to happen the most that very first year.

Seven months into the birth of our church-plant in Utah, Elevation Church, I began to question whether or not I had made the right decision. Things were hard. Things hadn't worked the way they were supposed to work. I was banged up a bit. I was worn out. Every job looked better than what I was doing. Why didn't that law school application get accepted?

I prayed every night.
*God, please let me do something else. Give me something else to just "know."*

## A Night to Remember

On April 30, the day after my oldest daughter turned one, we loaded up our blazer and hit the road to speak at a church in Colorado. Our church-plant still needed the financial help of supporting churches, so we made the eight-hour drive to raise funds.

We headed off early Saturday morning, my daughter securely strapped in the car seat behind the driver's seat and my wife in the front passenger's seat.

Up through Wyoming we made our voyage.

My wife and daughter quickly fell asleep in those early morning hours. I was watching the road with caution because it was raining hard.

As we got past Evanston, Wyoming, the interstate took us up a small mountain range. We were in the left-hand lane and had just passed a semitruck. The weather went from rain to snow in a matter of seconds.

I slowed down as we were heading up the incline of the mountain and decided to get into the right-hand lane. As I turned the wheel to the right, the blazer did something I have never felt a vehicle do in all my snow driving days in Utah. The back of the vehicle seemed to not want to leave the left side of the road.

We were heading up an incline sliding sideways with a semitruck heading straight for us. My mind immediately raced to thinking we are about to get hit by this semi.

But we didn't. Instead, our vehicle went off the right side of the road.

Problem was . . .

. . . there is NO side of the road.

Our vehicle violently rolled down the side of the mountain six times. It all happened so very fast, yet felt like super slow motion.

I gripped the steering wheel with everything I had and thought to myself: *Wow, you always wonder how you are going to die. This is it for me. Here it is. This is it.*

Ami woke up and threw her hands against the windows in sheer panic. I heard her gasp in all the air that was left in the blazer.

I quickly remembered that I wasn't alone—the two people I was called to look after in life, the two people I loved with everything in me, were in that blazer too!

I screamed out at the top of my lungs (I'm sure in my best eight-year-old girl voice), JESUS, S-A-V-E U-S!

Almost as soon as the words came out of my mouth our vehicle stopped.

We had landed at the bottom of this small little valley, right side up. Our vehicle was destroyed.

The top was caved in. The axle was half off on the side of the mountain. A tire was up there too. Windows were blown out. Car chargers had become missiles that were now literally stuck through the windshield. Our luggage was draped across the valley floor like a garage sale.

I immediately threw open the door and jumped out to get Madison out of the car seat behind me.

Ami's door was so badly damaged she had to crawl out my door.

Our family stood at the bottom of the valley floor next to our destroyed blazer just crying and holding each other.

By the time we walked up to the interstate, a highway patrolman was already there. An ambulance was on its way. A few cars had pulled over along with the semitruck.

I stood overlooking the valley and our vehicle.

(WOW! I should be in a Chevy Blazer commercial.)

I couldn't believe this had just happened to me. God had totally saved us. I had a small scratch on my hand that bled pretty good. Ami had one as well. I was in a little bit of shock, for sure.

Now, before I go any further for those of you who don't live near Wyoming, I need to explain that Wyoming has got to be one of the "whitest" places in the U.S. Now I know Idaho and Utah are up there, but Wyoming is pretty much straight vanilla.

So you can imagine my surprise at the miracle I was witnessing when I looked up from my staring contest with the valley floor to see an African-American man come walking down the interstate toward me. The thing that was really weird is that there was nowhere in particular he was walking from. No car to have emerged from, no city, no town, no rest stop . . . nothing.

This gentleman was dressed in an overly huge puffy winter coat, his hair was in cornrows, and he had a huge lip ring in the center of his bottom lip.

He walked right up to me and said, "I saw someone get thrown from your vehicle."

"No, sir, my family and I are okay. You probably saw my luggage getting shot out of the windows."

Nobody at the scene knew I was a follower of Jesus, let alone a church planter pastor.

He looked me straight in the eyes. "Satan is trying to shut you up. He wants you to stop. BUT, you can't stop man, you can't stop. God is going to protect you and guide you."

I stood there in shock.

Tears filled my eyes. I put my hand on his shoulder and said, "Thank you so much."

I slowly took my hand off of his shoulder and turned in the direction of where my wife was sitting and being looked after by the EMTs on scene. I turned back around . . .

. . . and he was gone.

I looked up and down the interstate.

Nothing.

Just white people.

Man, I hit my head hard.

I learned a few things that day.

One—my angel was black and had a piercing in his lip. That was cool.
Two—God was watching after my family and me.
Three—I knew what I was called to do, and God was giving me assurance.

Church planting is a full-contact sport of the spiritual and physical worlds. You will be subjected to all sorts of crazy situations you never even thought you would find yourself in. The only way you will make it through is if you are called by God to start a church. If you are not called, you will throw in the towel and just get out. Why would you WANT to be subjected to this craziness?

You can have all the junk I have to go through as a church planter, but I go through it 'cause I know I'm called to do this for God.

If you can see yourself doing anything other than church planting, go do it.

If you just know . . .

. . . then let the journey begin.

# Chapter One in Review

*Key Ideas*

1. Church planting is hard.
2. Only God can sustain the motivation of the person called to church planting.
3. God has a way of speaking to people about His desires for their lives. There is no "one size fits all" way to know God is speaking.
4. Church planting is a physical and spiritual full-contact sport.
5. If you aren't called to church planting, attempting it will chew you up and spit you out.

*Discussion Questions*

1. What is something that appears difficult that you think God might want you to do?
2. Describe a time when God has sustained you. How did you know it was God?
3. What do you wish God would tell you regarding His plans for your life?
4. Has there ever been a time when you started something for God but turned back because it was too much of a struggle? What happened?
5. Why do you think pursuing God's call for your life is so taxing physically and spiritually?

*Next Steps*

1. Describe God's vision for your life without regard for the complexity of the outcomes.

2. List some ways God is sustaining you right now.

3. Identify some things you are doing right now that you believe are part of God's plan for your life.

4. Complete this statement: I believe God has called me to _____. Even though it might be hard, I will not turn back because _____.

5. Pray for spiritual vitality and strength to pursue God's best for your life.

# CHAPTER 2

# IT'S ABOUT DISCIPLESHIP, STUPID

*"It is a gathering. Not a program. Not a building.
Not a business. Not a humanitarian outreach. Not a 501c3.
And definitely not a denomination."*

Before you plant a church, you need to really understand what is a *church* and what is the *purpose* of a church.

You look up the definition in any dictionary, or Google it for that matter, and you will get something like this: "a building where Christians meet for services."

Now—all of us will read that definition and say something to the effect that, "No way, that is not the definition. The secular world has it wrong."

BUT . . .

If we are honest (let's try to be as we walk through this book together), we might not claim that definition, but our definition is still messed up. Specifically in the way we practice . . .

The word *church* is translated from the Greek word *ekklēsia*. The definition of this word in the Greek is most generally translated to mean any public assembly.

Romans 16:5 states, "Greet also the church in their house." Paul uses the word *ekklēsia* to refer to a gathering of followers of Jesus that met in a house church. This would be a very small group of people.

Paul also used *ekklēsia* to refer to the followers of Jesus in an entire city (see 1 Corinthians 1:2 and 1 Thessalonians 1:1).

Luke, the medical doctor who wrote both the Gospel of Luke and Acts, used the word *ekklēsia* to refer to the followers of Jesus in a region. He wrote, "So the church throughout all Judea and Galilee and Samaria had peace and was being built up" (Acts 9:31).

The last use of the word *ekklēsia* we see in the New Testament is again used by Paul to refer to the followers of Jesus throughout the entire world. Commonly referred to as the "church universal," Paul wrote about how "Christ loved the church and gave himself up for her" (Ephesians 5:25).

So the word *ekklēsia*, which we translate as *church* means a group of followers of Jesus all the way from those in a house church, those in a city, those in a region, to those in the world.

Now that we have a background on what church is . . . No one can plant (start) a universal gathering of followers of Jesus. Followers of Jesus in a region maybe, over time if there is no one already in that region, and the same would go for followers of Jesus in an entire city. So we are thinking and talking about someone planting (starting) a smaller gathering of followers of Jesus, a smaller community within the larger gathering of the city, region, and world.

It is a gathering. Not a program. Not a building. Not a business. Not a humanitarian outreach. Not a 501c3. And definitely not a denomination.

### What Does a Local Gathering of Followers of Jesus Do?

Acts chapter two is one of the best places to gather information on what the local church is supposed to look like and be. Right after Jesus goes to heaven after His resurrection, His followers waited (per His instructions) for the Holy Spirit's empowerment, and the local gathering of Jesus' followers grew that day after the Holy Spirit empowered them. The end of Acts chapter two tells us how this new congregation acted as a local gathering of Jesus' followers.

"And they devoted themselves to the apostles' teaching and the fellowship, to the breaking of bread and the prayers. And awe came upon every soul, and many wonders and signs were being done through the apostles. And all who believed were together and had all things in common. And they were selling their possessions and belongings and distributing the proceeds to all, as any had need. And day by day, attending the temple together and breaking bread in their homes, they received their food with glad and generous hearts, praising God and having favor with all the people. And the Lord added to their number day by day those who were being saved." (Acts 2:42–47)

So here are the characteristics of a church according to this passage in Acts:

- Devotion to biblical teaching.
- Qualified leadership doing the biblical teaching (reference to the apostles).
- Fellowship (this word really means to gather together in a spirit of love and unity—not hanging out with people we really don't like, as it is often used today).
- Eating together (we don't share meals with those we hate—this is an intimate moment of "fellowship").
- Prayer.
- Temple meetings (regular gatherings in a public area).
- Giving to those in need.
- God's Spirit working through them.
  - *Unity.*
  - *Joyful and truthful hearts.*
  - *House meetings (regular small gatherings).*
  - *Worship of God.*
  - *And multiplication of more followers of Jesus.*

I wish so bad that I could go back in time to when we first planted Elevation Church. I had it all wrong.

I got caught up in the marketing aspect of church—which really was me being caught up in the characteristic of the regular public gatherings. There is nothing wrong with marketing, communication, and the large public gathering, but I missed the point.

In my mind, we were going to have four hundred people at our first service because we did a great job marketing this new exciting, awesome, fresh, young, hip church coming to town.

Who did I think those four hundred people were going to be? A bunch of people who didn't know Jesus?

I was crazy (and you are too) if you think a bunch of people who are not following Jesus are going to show up to your church-plant because you have a great service and a great graphic design artist. The truth is, you will get what we got.

158 people showed up.

Most of them from other churches. Other gatherings in our city. Followers of Jesus looking for a new home.

A few people who were not following Jesus showed up because their friends dragged them there.

But was that really the point of starting another church in our city? I am in Utah, and we don't have a lot of evangelical churches. It never crossed my mind to ask myself, *What is the point of planting a church?*

I was deflated after our first Sunday.

Four hundred people did not show up. Not that I knew who those four hundred people really should have been.

I was deflated because most of the people who showed up were already followers of Jesus—

"Church-hoppers."

In my spirit, I knew church planting wasn't about moving followers of Jesus from one church gathering to another.

I was missing the point, and most church plants do.

### Why Do We Need New Church-plants?

Hillary Swank starred in the 2007 movie *Freedom Writers,* which was based on the true story of high school teacher Erin Gruwell, who had helped to radically change the lives of a classroom full of students in Long Beach, California, two years after the L.A. riots. The movie focused in on the racial divides that existed at the school and how these thirty-odd students in one classroom overcame their natural order of fighting each other and falling on the streets to instead living as a family and graduating high school together.

It is a great movie.

We have seen these types of movies before. *Remember the Titans*–type movies. True. Human. Inspiring.

What hit me as I watched the movie wasn't the racial tension or socioeconomic plight of the students.

What hit me was how the other teachers depicted in the movie missed the point of the educational system.

I think we would all agree that schools exist to teach students. Teachers are trained on how to put together lesson plans, how to implement methods to foster response to those lesson plans and, ultimately, how to lead students to acquire new information that they hadn't possessed at the beginning.

Teachers are meant to teach new information to students.

But in this movie we see teachers who have lost that point. They feel more passionate about having a job. They feel more passionate about their lesson plans and methods, rather than if those methods are actually teaching anything to a certain segment of the school. These teachers have a mentality that the students need to WANT to learn—and if they don't WANT to learn, then you can't teach.

At one point in the movie, one of the other English teachers tells Hillary Swank's character that eventually those who don't want to learn will just stop coming to school. If she sticks around long enough, she will get to teach the upper classmen who WANT to learn.

It feels, at times, that this is what church planting has become.

We advertise with our mass mailers, give-aways, and "churchy branding" to our community. We focus on getting people to show up for a service, which is just one of the characteristics of a church. We miss the point of why new church-plants are needed.

The problem with focusing on one aspect or characteristic of a church is that the only people who will respond to that stuff are people who are already CHRISTIANS.

And in focusing on our large public gatherings, we have gotten into the business of wanting to pastor those who WANT to be taught and WANT a better church home than they currently have.

Frankly, church planting has turned into "Our church is better than your church, so JOIN US this SUNDAY for our LAUNCH SERVICE."

I have a friend who planted a church outside of a very large city. They decided to do some mass mailers to their community to promote their Sunday service where they were going to give out over fifty thousand dollars worth of prizes. Everything from a motorcycle to Plasma TVs.

850 people showed up.
Prizes were given out.
People were excited.

Next week came.
400 people showed up to service.

The next week.
300 people showed up to service.

The following week.
200 people showed up.

Is church planting about drawing the crowds to a service? This really is the perversion of the definition of a church, and only a small focus on one aspect of the characteristics of a church.

A crowd is not a church.

Anyone can draw a crowd.

I heard a very popular pastor say once that it was all about the service on Sunday. That all of our focus as pastors should be about having a great Sunday service. He even told us how he fired all of his staff members whose jobs didn't directly relate to the Sunday morning service. He went on to tell everyone that if we wanted to grow our churches, church-plants, etc., then we needed to focus on our Sunday services.

Let me be honest . . . If you go to church planting conferences or most of the training opportunities out there for church planting, you will find they largely focus on the latest and greatest church marketing techniques to draw people to your SERVICE.

Trying to get those who WANT to be there to your services. Making your SERVICE so amazing and marketable that people will want to come to it.

Newsflash: The only people who care about awesome and amazing services are those who grew up in church, have some church background, or are already going to church.

That's not even close to the point of church planting.

We are so focused on our methods and lesson plans that we forget the point is actually reaching people to disciple them. In our case, someone who doesn't know Jesus, finding Jesus, and growing in spiritual maturity with Him.

Jesus never told us to plant churches.

Nobody ever told me that.

Not once does Scripture command us to plant churches.

Not once.

Make sure you are not reading into this and thinking I am against church planting. I am the biggest fan of churches being planted. I love coaching church planters. I now just realize how too often we miss the point.

### Make Disciples or You Miss the Point

Jesus said in Matthew 28:19–20, "Go therefore and make disciples of all nations, baptizing them in the name of the Father and of the Son and of the Holy Spirit, teaching them to observe all that I have commanded you."

We are called to . . . scratch that . . . We were *commanded* to MAKE DISCIPLES.

Church planting should be the outgrowth of making disciples.

And what do disciples do when we get them together?
Healthy disciples will embody the characteristics we saw in the early church in Acts 2.

Let me sound really nerdy here for a minute. The Greek word Jesus uses for "go" in Matthew 28:19 modifies the imperative command "make disciples." When He says to go, He is commanding us to move with intention. Go is actually part of the command. In other words, Jesus says, "Your intention should be to make disciples. You are going to baptize them, and you are going to teach them the things I have taught you."

We were commanded to make disciples, not plant churches.
Churches being planted should happen because we are making disciples.

If you have taken a logic reasoning class in school you will learn that this process is a classic if-then statement, IF you make disciples, THEN you will have a church-plant. The reverse is not true though. If you have a church-plant, then you have disciples. It doesn't work that way and is logically flawed.

My mistake was not seeing this as the point.
Before you plant your church, you need to grab hold of this and cling to it with all you are.

The lesson plans and the teaching methods are important. They are not the point, though. The point is those who do not know Jesus coming to knowledge of Him.

Your intention should be to make disciples.

If you don't do this, you will create codependent Christian consumers who will eventually leave your church for the next Wal-Mart church that pops up in town. They will WANT you to serve them. They will WANT to consume. And their discipled life will be two inches deep and a thousand feet wide. The large public gathering will be all they care about. Even though U2 can pull off an amazing large public gathering, it doesn't make that event a church.

In the Old Testament, there is the story of Joshua.
I like Joshua.
He seems like a pretty good guy.
Having kids messed up my perception of him, though. Thanks to VeggieTales, in my mind he is a pickle that speaks with a harelip.

Joshua was discipled by none other than Moses.
How would you like Moses to be your mentor in life?

Joshua had the best leader to learn from. I would think that would make Joshua top shelf when it came to his own ability to lead people.

There was one glaring weakness in Joshua's life and leadership. He didn't disciple anyone. He didn't pass on what he had learned about following God.

In Judges 2:10 it says that a generation came along that didn't know God. Joshua missed the point.
It wasn't about leading to a physical destination.

It wasn't about the Promised Land.
It was about leading people TO GOD.

The Promised Land was a by-product of their dedication to God.

I wonder how the story would have been different had Joshua understood the point. His methods were good, his lesson plans were probably right on, but he didn't actually pass the information on to the next generation.

Four years into our church-plant, it was this very story of Joshua's legacy that jolted me out of missing the point.

What had we become?
What were we doing?

I had been creating a fan-base of consumers as though we were some sort of Vegas headlining show.

I pulled our leadership together and shared with them what we all knew from Scripture.
Our job should be about making disciples.
We had to be intentional about it.
We had to focus on it.
All of us.

And that is what we did.
Our whole staff, all our leaders, all our deacons . . . we all committed to making disciples.

I am talking a major cultural change within the church.

We gathered all of our spiritual mentors together for six weeks of training. It was like two-a-day football practices for getting us focused on what discipling was and what it wasn't.

We started preaching on what a disciple was supposed to look like.

We focused all our small groups and house churches on reproducing following Jesus in other people.

You know what happened?
Very slowly, but on purpose, I watched the people around me start to rely on God and not what I brought to the table. I started to watch people around me hear from God and engage with each other in the journey they found themselves on with Jesus. I watched all those characteristics of the church that are in Acts 2 just start to happen around me. I didn't have to force them or make them into a program of the church. I was the pastor, but Jesus became the LEAD.

I have seen more people come to Christ and the two-inch depth start to grow deeper for people since I dedicated myself and our church to making disciples.

Okay, so how do you do this in your church-plant before you launch?

**Going Deep**

Here is the plan I wish I had put into place at the onset of Elevation:

*1) Search Scripture and develop a rough sketch of what a disciple of Jesus looks like.*

This is important to understanding what you need to focus your discipleship on. The wheel doesn't have to be reinvented. There have been a lot of amazing followers of Jesus who have come before us and have figured out what a disciple looks like. We searched Scripture, we studied what others had come up with, and in the end we discovered the seven attributes of a follower of Jesus.

- A follower of Jesus will BE with Jesus—Surround yourself with His Bride, the church. Abide in His will. Read the sacred literature we call the Bible.
- A follower of Jesus will LISTEN to Jesus—Hear His commands through the Bible. Hear His words through prayer. Follow Jesus' leading through His Holy Spirit.
- A follower of Jesus will be HEALED by Jesus—Jesus brings reconciliation in our lives. He heals hurts, pains, perceptions, and even physical calamities.
- A follower of Jesus will INFLUENCE others for Jesus— Our lives are not our own and will be used to influence the world around us for Christ. We are SALT and LIGHT.
- A follower of Jesus will LOVE—Love God, love others.
- A follower of Jesus will PRAY to Jesus—Prayer becomes the central way in which we not only LISTEN but also communicate to our Lord through our journey here on Earth.
- A follower of Jesus will MANAGE—We might not be perfect, but the fruit of God's Spirit present in our lives will be evident as we mature in our walk with Christ.

*2) Commit to personally discipling others.*

If you believe it is about making disciples, it will be seen in the way you live your own personal life. If it is evident in your own personal life, then it will be easier to multiply through others. You cannot reproduce what you are not.

If you make it a program of the church, then it will just be a department. It will not be as important as Jesus tells us to make it, and it will eventually dry up without charismatic leaders driving the program.

Disciples are hand-crafted, not mass produced.

If you start at the beginning of the church planting process with leading someone to knowledge of Jesus and walking with them in their journey with Jesus, you will not only continue to do this for the life of the church but all of those who are now part of this new church will have this infused into the cultural DNA of your church.

We found that it worked best to set up weekly meetings with those we were discipling. A few of the people I am discipling e-mail, text, and call me throughout the week. We meet up for a more formal sit down every other week. I try not to disciple more than three people at a time. More than that, and I don't give those I am discipling adequate attention.

We also found that once someone comes to know Jesus, we need to outline and agree to goals at the beginning of the process:

- To see them grow in their spiritual maturity with Jesus.
- To turn around and disciple someone else.

The discipleship process was actually multiplied over time instead of a bunch of leaders doing all the discipling. Jesus spoke the Great Commission to His disciples, but Matthew recorded it for all of us who are following Jesus. It isn't a pastor's job—it is a Christian's job.

Get this in your head now—it is everyone's job to disciple someone. Teach it to those you pastor at the beginning and you will see this lived out in the depth of the new Jesus community.

There are a lot of great books on what a discipled relationship looks like and what a healthy spiritual disciple is. Invest in these books at the beginning of your church planting journey, not in the middle or end.

*3) Don't recruit people to be part of the early church planting process who will not commit to discipling others.*

This goes back to reproducing who you are, not what you are not. During the beginning stages of the church, if you recruit a team or people who don't embrace this as the point of church planting, it will not be the focus of your church.

*4) Develop a discipleship pathway.*

At some of the church planting boot camps I have been part of, they will usually walk you through a discipleship map. The premise is to develop a plan to move non-Christians to become believers who develop into mature followers of Jesus. This map will generally consist of taking all the programs of the church and finding out at what stage of a person's spiritual growth they play into. This is a great exercise to determine if you are missing programs or events at these significant stages.

Here is why I don't like the map.

Most of the church planters I see take all the things that they have seen and heard at another church and just try to do them at their new church. This just categorizes them on this map. However, none of these events were designed with the intent of doing what they were now categorized for.

It should almost be reversed.

Don't think of what a group or an organization can do. Think of what an individual can do to lead another individual to Christ and the steps it would take for them to help others become a mature follower of Christ. And then for those people to repeat the process on their own. Of course, you will have to come up with the ideal situation that will probably never happen exactly the same way every time, but it will give you at least a blueprint to work with as you and your team start to disciple others. Think of it like a football or basketball play. You draw up how it is supposed to happen and then if it doesn't play out the intended way during the actual execution, you still know what your end goal is. You try to follow it as close to perfect as you can, but you realize it might not happen that way.

If you have a pathway set up before you do anything else, everything you do as a church-plant will have the DNA of disciple making intertwined into the culture of the new church.

Find people in your community who don't know Jesus.

Teach them about Him.

Disciple them.

Baptize them.

Teach them to follow Jesus as you are following Him.

When you get enough of them around you, then you have a church-plant.
But please don't miss the point.

# Chapter Two in Review

*Key Ideas*

1. The church is a gathering of believers, not a program, business, humanitarian outreach, nonprofit organization, or denomination.
2. The church was established to create authentic, God-honoring community.
3. Many churches define success in terms of the number of bodies in attendance.
4. Anyone can draw a crowd. Yet few in the crowd are from the unchurched portion of the local community.
5. The purpose of the church is to make disciples. Because we want instant viability, we often coax people into outperforming their level of spiritual maturity. That's not discipleship; that's manipulation.

*Discussion Questions*

1. Think back on your perception of the church. How has your understanding of the church changed?
2. What do you want the primary characteristic of your church to be?
3. What is your definition of success? What should be the real measure of a church's success?
4. How can your church be more effective in reaching the unchurched in your community?
5. Why is drawing people from other congregations often counter-productive for new church-plants?

*Next Steps*

1. Spend some time in the Bible studying the biblical characteristics of the church.
2. Begin developing a mission or purpose statement for a new church.
3. Determine how your church will measure success and then develop a plan to produce disciples.
4. Talk to unchurched people in your community and ask them why they don't attend church.
5. Begin developing a framework for establishing a church that is more appealing to the unchurched than to church-hoppers.

# CHAPTER 3

# STOP COPYING—YOU'RE NOT XEROX

*"The methods for bringing people to God are not sacred,
but the message is."*

"You are a church planter, huh? So, what model are you using?"
"What?"
"What model will your church be?"
"Aaaaahhhhh . . . maybe like Nikki Taylor—young looking, hip, and
fashionable, but mature."

I can't tell you the number of times I was asked about the model
we would be using for our church. I had no clue what anyone was
talking about. I thought for sure that they had all lost their minds.

My real answer had to do with us being a church that preached
the Word of God, loved people, worshiped God together in house
churches and large gatherings, and served the community.

That answer still didn't seem to give my inquisitors the answer they
were looking for. In fact, it only led to them trying to put us in
some category: seeker, house church, attractional, etc.

Who takes you serious without a "model"?

I mean, if you pick the wrong model, then some church planting groups will reject you, others will embrace you, and others will call you heretics.

## The Message Is Sacred, Not the Methods

In Luke chapter 14, Jesus tells a parable about a big party that a man was once throwing. The man sends his servant out to talk to the invited party guests at the time of the party. The invited guests give a series of excuses of why they can't make it to the party.

"I just bought some property and need to examine my new purchase."
"I just bought some cattle and need to check them out."
"I have a new wife who is super high maintenance, please forgive me for not coming."

The servant reports everything back to his party-throwing boss. This boss becomes very angry and tells the servant to go get all the poor, crippled, and lame of the city—those who are outcasts—and invite them to fill up the party.

The servant again returns to tell the boss that what he has requested has been done, but there is still room at the party for more people.

The boss looks at his servant and says one of the most telling things found in a parable.

"Go out to the highways and hedges and compel people to come in, that my house may be filled" (Luke 14:23).

COMPEL them.

The methods for bringing people to God are not sacred, but the message is.

Models will change over time, but the message never will.

You should not spend your time and energy trying to master a model or method. There are bigger questions:

What does God want to do in your city?
Are you making disciples?
Are you getting people INTO the kingdom of God?
Are you compelling?
Are you working to see people find JESUS?

Let me offer a word of caution: the party/banquet in this parable is not to be seen as a service; it is representative of the kingdom of God.

## Models

There is a huge list of models you can try to emulate, but if you do, then you are not allowing God to work through you, instead becoming a Xerox of what God did through someone else. Making disciples is not a program to be Xeroxed or microwaved. It will take different methods in different cities, but you will only find what it takes by getting out into your city and DOING something.

Success is our worst enemy in the church world.

As soon as we are successful, then our methods are elevated to publicized fame, and we find ourselves in the franchise business rather than the disciple business.

Seriously. Think of all the church conferences out there.
We put the methods and those that run them on a shelf for all to try to learn from when, in reality, they were not the reasons why something worked in the first place. It was the heart to reach people and find something/anything that would COMPEL them to come into the kingdom.

Just searching the word *church* on Amazon.com gave me a bunch of books on the first page that all were methods/models of church.

*Total Church*
*Simple Church*
*Transformational Church*
*Deep Church*
*Sticky Church*

These are great books with some good insights, but they become "porn" to our call to make disciples and the existence of the church. It becomes fantasy of what could be rather than what God is asking us to be.

The methods are not sacred.

One of my favorite movies is the *Multiplicity.* In the movie, Michael Keaton's character clones himself twice. Then his clone makes a clone of himself. The clone of the clone is called Number 4.

Number 4 is slow mentally, socially, and doesn't produce anything good other than comedy in the film.

Church planters who focus on modeling their church after another are making clones of a clone. Bus ministry, early morning prayers, baseball diamond structured classes, 24-hour prayer, cell ministry, movie theater church, etc. These were all successful ministries that were original at one time to a local church to reach their community for Jesus.

We are to clone ourselves after Jesus, not others.
Maybe He will lead us to use methods outlined above, but we don't go looking for methods first.

"Oh, that looks like fun. I want to do it that way."

## Mindsets

I am no church scholar, but I think there are mindsets we have in our view of the local church that differ from models of the church. I also think it is important to understand our own perception of how we view the role of the church in the community so that we understand how we will see ourselves making disciples and growing the church.

I don't think every church will fall into just one of these mindsets; you will probably see your view of the church hit at least two of these mindsets in ministering and making disciples.

Mindsets of the local church include . . .

*Service.* View of the church as an instrument of serving the community through community projects, programs, correcting the wrongs of the social injustices around the world, and continually seeking to become a functioning partner with the local city/county/state. Food banks, financial classes, random acts of kindness, community convoys, parenting classes, community cleanup, behavior addiction classes, divorce recovery groups, missions trips, local community projects, etc.

*Redemption.* View of the church as an instrument of redeeming the city by its presence as the bride of Christ. The city is redeemed by God because the local church exists and is in the city. Example: God sparing the cities of Sodom and Gomorrah because there were just a few righteous people.

*Community.* View of the church as an instrument to create an environment for fellowship of those who belong to the family of God. This mindset usually is big on creating a strong identity and loyalty to the church as a whole and uses terms like "family" and "fellowship" in their terminology more than other churches.

*Institution.* View of the church as an institution in which a hierarchy of leadership and disciples are produced and followed. The church is lifted to a higher level of esteem than in other church mindsets, and leaders are seen as having special ordination and authority from God. This view sees salvation coming not only from Jesus, but also through the church as an organization.

*Prophet.* View of the church as a mouthpiece to proclaim the truth of God to the city and the world. The church is given the rights and authority by God to preach and teach. This view of the church puts a high priority in speaking publicly and often to the world about what God believes and says on a certain subject.

Once you have understood how you view the local church in the discipling process, then you can start to ask God what methods He would want you to use when working within the city you are called to plant a church. No single model for discipling and no single mindset for viewing the church is perfect. Don't get caught up in thinking you "can't do it that way."

In the same way the older stuck-in-the-mud churches have a hard time changing because someone always says, "We never did it this way before." Don't get caught in that same mindset when you look at the church you are planting and you start to see what God is calling you to do. Don't catch yourself saying, "I've never seen it done like that before."

Be YOU in this process.

I even think this goes to naming the church. Don't Xerox the name of your favorite church or the personality of the pastor you idolize. The name of your church should speak to who and what you are as a new group of disciples of Jesus.

Here are some tips in picking a church name. I wish someone would have gone over this with me in detail before we started:

1. Listen if God is speaking to you about a specific name. Spend some time praying and asking God for direction.

2. Avoid copying.

As I stated earlier, don't copy other good church names out there. Google search local church names in your area and state. Try to be as original as you possibly can, especially in your city and state. You get into legal trouble when you start copying names as well. Is there a trademark on the name? Did you search the state business name database to see if your name is already taken or a very close one exists?

3. Avoid generic names, difficult names, long names, and *Christianese* terminology.

You don't want to name yourself something that is so generic that you just sound like the run-of-the-mill church that someone saw in another state when they were growing up.

Be you.

The name of the church will express to the public (Christian and non-Christian) who you are. It will be your first impression. Are you generic, or are you something special? Don't have a difficult name that no one can pronounce or understand. Using Greek or Latin words sounds awesome to those of us who have a Christian background but can be hard to pronounce for the average non-follower of Jesus.

And of course . . . I hate having to say it . . . but stay away from names that might mean one thing to one culture or group and an entirely different thing to the people you're trying to reach. Know your audience. While it might say one thing to a follower of Jesus, it might say something completely different to a non-follower.

The "Got Milk?" campaign that we are so aware of in the United States was launched in Mexico. The problem is the translation in Spanish—"Are You Lactating?"—Didn't have the same effect on one group as it did on the other.

4. Wordplay.
We came up with Elevation Church in 2004. (That was before Elevation Church in North Carolina. Just wanted to get that in writing. But you could look up the incorporation papers of both, if you wanted.)

We came up with the name by thinking of all the words we liked for a church name and then looking through a thesaurus. Find a dictionary. Search the Internet. Look through a thesaurus. But play with words to help get your creative juices flowing.

5. Name should speak of who you are and who you are not.
This goes back to number three. The name should reflect what this new church-plant is about. If you are not very hip and creative, don't pick a name that communicates you are. If you are not young and vibrant, don't pick a name that leads people to believe this. Find something that IS you. If you have a name like Vibe Church and you wear suits and ties to church, I would think you made a mistake in your name.

6. Assign two or three people to help you.
Don't get a huge group of people to help with this process. The more people you get involved, the more opinions you will pile into the process. Avoid doing it by yourself, as you do want to get other

perspectives, but at the end of the day you will need to be the one to make a decision. I have heard stories of church-plants just hiring companies to name them based on questionnaires they fill out. This can be very expensive. If you have the money, knock yourself out. But I think you can do it on your own.

7. Keep it simple.
Don't overdo the name. Simple is better. You don't need to have a church name that is so complex that eventually people, even the people in your church, come up with a nickname for the church to stay away from your complex name.

8. Stay away from names that place your church in a location.
Don't name your church after the street where you meet or the place—8th Street Baptist Church is a real church name, but they are now located on 51st Street. Movie Theater Church sounds great, but what if you have to move out of the movie theater? I even suggest staying away from city names if you can help it. What if you have to move out of the city or move to the city next door?

9. Brand your name.
There are a lot of books on color theory and what design communicates. Once you pick a name, explore these ideas and pick colors, logos, graphics, and symbols that flow with the name. Slap your name on everything you possibly can and start to develop your identity in connection with your name. When someone hears about [INSERT CHURCH-PLANT NAME], they will think about you.

We hired a company to develop this for us once we picked a name. It is a lot cheaper than getting an actual name from a company. It worked really well for us, and we were very pleased.

10. Website.

The first thing your church name should be slapped on is a website of some sort. You will get what you pay for, so think of what you want your name to communicate when someone sees it, and what the website will communicate as well. At the beginning of a church-plant, a simple splash page is a great way to start to get your name out there for the digital world.

Here are some bad church names based on the above advice not followed:

- The Church of I Am THAT I AM (Should we pick a name that non-followers of Jesus are guaranteed to not understand?)
- Beaver Lick Christian Church (Did a teenager name this church?)
- Boring United Methodist Church (Seriously. The only people who get this are those who live in Boring, MD.)
- Little Hope Baptist Church (Did they expect anyone to show up? I feel like we should church-plant in this church.)
- Hell for Certain (I'm not kidding.)
- Hole in the Roof Christian Church (Well, get it fixed . . . oh, the story of the guy coming through the hole in the roof to Jesus . . . I just got it!)

On the other hand, here are some great church names based on the above advice:

- Plum Creek Community Church (The name comes from the county the church is located in.)
- Soul City Church
- The Orchard
- The Village
- ONE Community Church
- K2 the Church
- Elevation Church (Excuse the self-promotion. When you write your book, you can include your church's name too.)

Be who God called you to be and not anyone else. You weren't designed to clone another church.

Compel them to come in.

# Chapter Three in Review

*Key Ideas*

1. The message is sacred; the methods are ever changing.
2. It is more important to know what God wants to do rather than how other churches are doing it.
3. Success can be an enemy of the church.
4. Different churches have different mindsets. Knowing yours is vital.
5. A church name should communicate with the unchurched in a way that invites them inside.

*Discussion Questions*

1. What are some things you've seen done in the church that you would like to see stopped?
2. What does God want to do in your city? Why aren't other churches doing it?
3. Explain how success can be the enemy of the new church.
4. Review the list of mindsets on page 44. How would you describe your mindset? How would you describe the mindset of your church?
5. What are you trying to communicate through your church name?

*Next Steps*

1. Define five non-negotiable elements of a new church.
2. Clearly state your understanding of God's vision for your new church.

3. Make the vision for reaching your community part of every communication piece.
4. Communicate your mindset to the leadership team for your church.
5. Begin identifying possible church names.

# CHAPTER 4

# PROFESSIONAL ATHLETES GOT NOTHING ON THE CONFIDENCE OF A CHURCH PLANTER

*"Lack of confidence will keep you from attracting those God has called you to lead."*

Doctor Charles Ridley came up with thirteen factors (qualities) for successful church planters. It has become one of the standard measuring tools for most church planting groups across the world. Many church planting organizations take Ridley's list and modify it based on their own organizational experiences and studies. His list continues to be one of the most popular outlines of the essential ingredients to being a church planter. (Just Google "Charles Ridley 13" and you'll see what I mean.)

When I started the church-planting journey, my church planting organization required me to do a church planting assessment with a certified church-planting assessor. I had no idea what we were going to be asked or how we would be assessed. At the time, I didn't ask, either.

I recommend an assessment to anyone that wants to plant a church. I am sure your church planting group or denomination has something you can use. Our assessment lasted almost seven hours in a conference room. It was basically a really long interview. (My wife, Ami, was eight months pregnant at the time, so it probably could have been a shorter meeting, but pregnant women need to pee a lot.)

About a month after that, our church-planting director called to tell us that we passed the assessment with very high scores. I had no idea what the standard was for us to pass. About five years ago, I was asked to be part of that same church-planting group that had assessed me. After the first meeting, I asked for my assessment that was given so many years back. I then was able to ask all the questions I had never asked about assessing back when we started our process.

I came to find out that our church planting organization used Dr. Ridley's 13 factors to assess new church planters. I had a fun time reading through each of Ridley's factors and what our assessor thought of us in each of the categories after our interview.

Here is what shocked me.

Of all the books I had read on church planting and the boot camps and conventions I had attended, I had never encountered such wisdom that was found in Dr. Ridley's qualities and factors. Why was I finally learning about these things after all of these years? They needed to be taught to potential church planters.

The great news is I have seen a surge in teaching of these factors and really making sure they are being communicated early on in a potential church planters journey. For easy reference, here are Dr. Ridley's 13 factors:

## 1. Vision Capacity

Ridley defined this as having the ability to project into the future beyond the present. A church planter must be able to sell this projection of the future to those he is leading and working with as well as establishing a very clear church culture identity that is related to that vision.

## 2. Intrinsically Motivated

A church planter should be able to work long, hard, and be a self-starter. If you can't build something from nothing, you will trip in the process.

## 3. Creates Ownership of Ministry

This quality almost goes hand in hand with vision capacity. A church planter has to not just sell the vision, but also get people to feel responsible for that vision, for discipleship, and the health of the new church community.

## 4. Relates to the Unchurched

This is the ability to communicate publicly and personally in a style that is understood by those who are not followers of Jesus. It goes beyond just communication through both speech and body language—it speaks of WANTING to connect, not being afraid to connect, and breaking down barriers to connect with those who are not in a church community and not following Jesus.

## 5. Spousal Cooperation

A church planter and spouse should understand the roles that they will both play in the process of starting a new Jesus community.

The couple should have evaluated the consequences of church planting and what effect ministry will have on their family and children. It really boils down to good communication between the church planter and spouse on what is going to happen as they move forward and that they are both on board with those plans.

6. *Effectively Builds Relationships*
Ridley identified that a church planter needed to have the ability to display God's love and compassion to people when they express needs and concerns. Helping others feel secure and comfortable, not responding judgmentally or prejudicially, should mark healthy relationships for church planters.

7. *Committed to Church Growth*
This goes back to our second chapter in our discussion on disciples—a church planter needs to be committed to spiritual and relational growth of the new church community. Recognizing that non-growth is threatening and self-defeating, a church planter should see this church project within the larger context of God's kingdom.

8. *Responsive to Community*
You have to understand your community and the culture of that community. A church planter has to be able to identify and assess the needs of that community. It isn't about being a complete community need-fixer, but to understand how to use the resources of the new church community, how the church ministry will adapt to the character of the community, and to not confuse the larger community as the church community.

## 9. Utilizes Giftedness of Others

Church planters can't do it alone. You need to learn to release and equip others to lead the church community. The leader of the church-plant needs to discern the spiritual gifts of others and be able to delegate effectively in areas of ministry.

## 10. Flexible and Adaptable

This isn't easy. You have to be able to cope with ambiguity, constant (even abrupt) change, and be able to shift priorities and emphases during those times effectively.

## 11. Builds Group Cohesiveness

As disciples are being made, a church planter needs to be able to incorporate theses new disciples into the already developed group of followers of Jesus. As the church community continues to grow, the different groups within the larger church community need to feel connected to each other and the overall vision. A church planter keeps all of this as one and monitors the morale of the people in the church.

## 12. Resilience

Church planters need to overcome setbacks without defeat, expect the unexpected, and rebound from loss.

## 13. Exercises Faith

As I discussed in chapter one, you have to possess a conviction from God to walk in this church-planting journey. Church planting demands miracles and God's favor. You need to believe in both and expect them both.

Every item in Dr. Ridley's list boils down to one thing. Without this one thing, it is very difficult for any of these 13 qualities to take root and contribute to the success of the church-plant and the church planter. What is that one thing?

Confidence.

At the end of the day, being a successful church planter is about having the confidence to make key decisions. If you don't have the confidence to cast vision, motivate others, relate to the unchurched, and build relationships, then you will ultimately fail.

Confidence keeps you shooting the basketball in game seven of the finals when you haven't made a shot all game.

Confidence keeps you throwing the football deep when you have already thrown five interceptions.

Confidence keeps you swinging the bat with bases loaded even when you are batting .000 for the game.

Church planting, as we have already gone over, is about making disciples. Leading others into an unknown area of life—following Jesus—must be done with confidence. The facts and figures of following Jesus are in front of people every day. The books are there. But these do not lead people.

People lead people.

People inspire others to move.

Those who inspire us and lead us do so with self-confidence.

A guy I had known for almost ten years came to me one day to talk about him being a church planter. I didn't need to sit him down and go through Ridley's thirteen factors. I knew this guy in and out almost immediately. He talked to me about his passion to plant a church. He talked to me about reaching lost people. He talked to me about what God had called him to do. He talked to me about community involvement.

He finished talking and looked at me. "What do you think?"

"Well, I think this will be hard for you to hear, but you are very unconfident in life in general. You gave me a qualifier for everything you told me and constantly backtracked statements to make sure that if I didn't like the answer, you had a plan B. All of this points to your lack of confidence in what you would be doing as a church planter."

He stared at me for a little while, lowered his head, and then dropped his voice. "You are right. I want to do this, but I am not confident in any of this. I am worried I would make a mistake and am making a mistake. I was hoping that if you told me this was from God that I would gain confidence."

I reached over and lifted his head up, as a father might do to his little boy. I looked him in the eyes and said, "Joe, God gives us boldness when the Holy Spirit is upon us. When He is leading you, you will have that confidence you need. You need to learn to walk in what you know is true and not what you wonder is. I am not saying you will never be a leader because of your lack of confidence now, I am telling you that God can give it to you, can teach it to you, and will use you."

Now the opposite has happened in my life too. A new church planter wanted to go to lunch with our worship leader and me. I love hearing the vision that God has given to these church plants for Utah, so of course I said yes. Our time with the new church planter was fun, encouraging, and it was good food too.

On our way home, I turned to our worship leader and asked him what he thought of the new church-plant and the planter.

"Well, he is very confident. I think he is his biggest fan."
I smiled and pondered this insight. "I don't think this guy will fail."

There is just something about confidence.
Confidence in what God has called you to do.
Confidence in the gifts God has given you.
Confidence in God.

I believe that confidence for a church planter comes when we realize how dependent we are on God and how dependent the church is on God. It is in this vein that we need to inject ourselves.

Let me give you an example here.

My daughters are the joy of my life. Each one of them could be labeled a daddy's girl. When they are scared, hurt, or unsure of what to do next; they end up running into my arms. Berlyn, my youngest, will say to me, "I want to hold you." I pick them up, put them on my lap, and almost immediately their security tank is refilled. And when that happens, their confidence level is as high as it can be. They are ready to take on the world. I can tell my daughters to do what they normally wouldn't have the confidence to do because of how safe and secure they feel, believing not only that they can do it but that they cannot fail.

Our confidence must come from this reliance on God.

Out of all the church planters I have trained and coached, I see the confident ones as usually being the most successful in leading a growing community of new disciples of Jesus. I think it goes along with what Craig Groeschel calls having "IT"—that something that makes you a successful church planter. Maybe that "IT" is the favor of God that comes from reliance on God.

I know that when we started our church-planting journey, depending on the day you caught me, I could seem unconfident about the decisions I was making and questioning whether we really were following what God had said.

Confidence is what I lacked internally.

I am sure I showed it to those around me, because I was really intentional in making sure I didn't show any weakness to those I was leading. Yet, I was unconfident in each decision I was making. I was second-guessing myself. I was looking over my shoulder. It came back to being so caught up doing ministry that I wasn't spending time hearing from God.

When I sit down with new church planters now, I focus on confidence.

Is this what you are supposed to be doing?
Do you believe God has called you?
Do you believe God has gifted you for this project?
Do you believe God has called you to lead this?

Lack of confidence will cause your new church-plant to stumble through early planning stages and will hold you back from leading others.

Lack of confidence will keep you from attracting those God has called you to lead.

Lack of confidence will keep you from relying on God and finding manmade programs to rely on.

Let me tell you a story from the Bible that really illustrates this idea. The way the early followers of Jesus dealt with confidence helped me to learn what it means to be a confident leader for God.

*Principle 1: Make a decision and go with it.*

We all know the story about the disciples sitting on the boat when they see what they say is a ghost walking on the water toward them. They realize it is Jesus.

Peter was a bold man; he spoke his mind and acted on his emotions. He was most likely the oldest of all the disciples, with the natural ability to be looked up to by the other disciples, which probably helped him to step up to the plate more than once. Peter gets out of the boat and with Jesus' encouragement begins to walk on the water to Him.

But . . .

He starts to sink into the water.

He panics.

He starts to splash around.

And Jesus has to pull him up.

What happened?

Peter was given a direction from Jesus and had that direction set. But when he took his eyes off Jesus, his confidence was lost. He began to think of all the logical things of walking on water.

You were not supposed to be able to walk on water.

No one else was doing it this way.

What would happen if he got too far from the boat and couldn't get back?

I can't swim if this doesn't work!!!

When God calls you to do something, make the decision and go with it. When you start to second-guess yourself in that decision, you lose confidence and you *will* sink. All of that second-guessing doesn't just take away confidence, but it also bogs down the task at hand.

*Principle 2: You will make mistakes.*

Peter made countless mistakes.

He told Jesus that He didn't have to endure the cross.
Cut a dude's ear off.
Sank while walking on water.
Denied Jesus three times.

What I love is that just one of those could have completely stalled out Peter's confidence from ever attempting anything else in life.

Did it?
Nope.

Peter stepped right back up to the plate.

He might have struck out five times, but when he was given the chance to bat again, he swung for the fence. Failure was part of the journey, and Peter didn't let that stop his confidence.

Peter isn't told to address the crowd that had gathered at the day of Pentecost, but when the opportunity came for someone to address what the Holy Spirit was doing in the lives of the followers of Jesus, Peter stood up and with confidence became a testimony to who Jesus was. This is a man who a little over a month and a half before didn't even admit to being associated with Jesus. Now we see him walking in confidence.

You will make mistakes in planting a church.

Everyone does.

Mark Driscoll did. Mark Batterson did. Erwin McManus did. Francis Chan did. And you will too.

Don't let the mistakes dictate your confidence. Simply admit them, be transparent, and move on. It's just part of the journey.

Pretending you don't make mistakes is arrogance and will kill your leadership. Don't pretend you are perfect, but don't let the imperfection hurt your confidence.

I have made so many mistakes as a leader. (Telling the publisher that I could write this book in the time I told them is one, but we don't need to talk about that.)

I remember at the early stages of planting the church putting a former pastor in the speaking/teaching schedule for our Sunday service. It was a huge mistake. The guy was terrible. People left scratching their heads. What did he just say? I had to go back to our leadership team and answer for my judgment call on that one. I didn't mind saying I had made a mistake, but it didn't ever stop me from making other judgment calls on other speakers for our Sunday teachings.

We borrowed the idea from others during the initial stages of planting our Jesus community, and it really has helped our whole team understand and overcome failure. (I think Mark Batterson said it to me first, so I will give him the credit here.) Here it is:

*Principle 3: Everything is an experiment.*

If it doesn't work, it's okay. It was an experiment.

In fact, I pulled a bunch of our staff together when I was putting notes together for this chapter and asked them what were my biggest failures as a leader that I could share in this book. Our media director, who has been with our church-plant since day one, said, "Since everything is an experiment, I don't know if any of us has ever failed. Things didn't work, and we did something different."

*Principle 4: Believe "the buck stops here."*

As a leader, you will need to sometimes have the final say on a situation. There is no such thing as having three different people who have the final say. It doesn't work like that. Someone has to be out in front leading. And there will come decisions that are tough that no one wants to make, but you have got to make them.

We started Elevation Church as a co-pastored church.
Worked great at first.
Had its rough moments.
It was a mistake, at least for us.

I co-pastored and co-founded Elevation Church with one of my best friends, Ryan Lind. We are still really good friends to this day. He didn't leave the church because of the co-pastoring situation; he was called by God to pastor in Ohio. This was a great move since, as a big Denver Broncos fan, I knew God didn't yet dwell in Cleveland because of all those prayers that were thrown up against John Elway back in the day.

Bottom line, I have personally seen how a church can get bogged down with having two people feeling like they have the final say on something.

Ryan and I are completely different but usually came to the same conclusion. There were times I would have handled things way different then he did and vice versa. It wasn't hard for us to work through these things, but I saw who it didn't work for was those we were leading. People basically picked one of us as the "leader" in their minds. When the other one of us would make a decision that didn't gel with them, they would run to the other. Almost like pitting parents against each other, hoping for the answer they wanted.

There needs to be ONE leader, and that ONE leader needs to understand that they will sometimes be called on because of the situation to make a "buck stops here" decision.

Peter and Paul both understood this, not just in who they were as leaders, but by the very nature of leadership. In Acts 15, they show up to a council of leaders to give their opinions on Gentiles who are now following Jesus. They both realize that they are not the central leaders in this decision but are giving their views.

By the end of the council, when a decision is given, James is the leader who makes the call, of course with the counsel of other leaders. His "buck stops here" call is that Gentiles do not have to be circumcised, but they should follow the dietary restrictions of the Jews so they could have good relationships with them. I even love the way James says it: "For it has seemed good to the Holy Spirit and to us . . ." (Acts 15:28).

He says that their decision is based on what they feel God is leading them to do and what they see as right. I like that there is this implication from James that they might be wrong, but this is the decision they are making.

James is part of making a decision that will have a lasting effect on millions of people. His confidence helps him to make a huge decision.

Peter and Paul accept the decision and move on.

*Principle 5: Have a "I will not fail" attitude.*

No matter what is thrown at you, confidence will keep you going.

Paul can tell you this.

Thrown in prison.
Beaten.
Shipwrecked.
Persecuted.
Run out of town.
Alienated.
Mocked.

Nothing stopped him. He was confident in what God had called him to do, what his gifts from God were, and who he was in Christ.

Confidence will propel you through tough times.
Confidence will say there is a way when everything else says you hit a dead end.
Confidence will always find a way.

Two things helped me to overcome my lack of confidence while planting a church.

My time with God. And getting a mentor and coach in my life.

A mentor and a coach are not the same thing.

A mentor is someone we can ask questions of and learn from. Someone you look up to in his or her ministry or life. I have three different mentors, and I make sure that each month I spend time talking to them and asking lots of questions. I process my thoughts and directions from God with my mentors and gain great insight into what God is asking me to do. The more informed I feel, the more confident I am. This may not be true for you, but this worked for me.

A mentor most likely already exists in your life; you need to identify who that is and ask him or her to serve in this capacity with you. If you verbalize this relationship as a mentor relationship, then it will keep you accountable to making that connection.

To help you identify a mentor, look for this type of person in your life:

Someone you look up to.
Someone from whom you are certain of gaining advice in ministry and life.
Someone you feel is farther along in the journey than you find yourself.
Someone you will listen to.
Someone you believe in.
Someone who knows you and understands you.
Someone who is godly and follows God first above all else.
Someone who is not a new follower of Jesus, but someone who is mature in his or her faith.

A coach is very different than a mentor.

A coach, as is implied in his or her title, is someone who will coach you along the journey. You don't ask coaches questions; they ask you questions. Coaches help you process decisions by pulling the information out of you, not giving it to you. Every great sports player always had a coach on the sideline who could see the field of play from a different point of view. Such coaches could never do what the athlete was doing, but their point of view and insight helped their players process the information of the game. You need someone to help question your decisions and help you process the information of church planting. Coaches will hold you to goals you set, assist you in creating action plans, and will help you process strategically before you bring things to your team.

Coaching has become the buzzword in the business and church world. More and more people are being certified and trained to coach pastors and leaders. Most church planting organizations today will assign you a coach or require you to have a coach if you are going to plant a church with them. This wasn't the case when I went out to plant a church. I didn't seek a church planting coach until almost three years into planting. It was by far one of the best decisions I made. My church planting coach was a professional coach who had coached lots of church planters. Almost immediately I had someone to talk to once a month who didn't have the answers, just questions for me. He helped to pull the answers out of me. My confidence grew as I spent time processing with my coach. He helped me to set goals, and he was the one who followed up on me to see where I was with my goals.

There is only one tip I would give you in picking a coach. Hopefully you will pick a coach who has experience and training, but you need to pick someone who you can connect with relationally.

Now a coach will usually cost you money. A mentor usually will not. Budget for a coach, and get both a coach and mentor BEFORE you set out on your church-planting journey.

Let me end this chapter with this: I have given you the qualities of a successful church planter, the foundation for those qualities, the principles of that foundation of confidence, and ways to increase your confidence through mentors and coaches . . . but what are the qualities that will derail a church-plant?

## Things That Disqualify Church Planters

Let me share with you what I think are all quality "stoppers" for church planters. It is a short list of four—three of them I took from Dr. J. Allen Thompson and his dissertation on *Assessing Church Planters*.

*Stopper #1—Lack of Confidence*
Everything we have been talking about in this chapter.

*Stopper #2—Arrogance*
Overconfidence. Displaying conceit. Thinking that you will not and cannot make a mistake.

*Stopper #3—Betraying Trust*
Breaking confidence with others when they trust you. Destroying the confidence that others have in you.

*Stopper #4—Immoral and Unethical Lifestyle*

Living on the margins of moral standards and values. Not having confidence in God and His truth for life.

These are the deal breakers I look for in church planters. These are the deal breakers I look for in myself. If these start to rear their ugly heads, I am quick to submit to godly men in my life to help me get back on track. My coach and mentors keep me aware of these stoppers in my life.

Confidence is the foundational element on which all the qualities of a church planter grow. If you don't spend time increasing your confidence or improving your confidence, your church-plant will suffer and limp along.

# Chapter Four in Review

*Key Ideas*

1. Dr. Charles Ridley developed a list of 13 factors by which church planters are evaluated.
2. One key to church planting is confidence.
3. True confidence is the result of one's reliance on God.
4. Church planters must make certain decisions, admit mistakes, take responsibility, and exhibit determination.
5. Church planters will be undermined by a lack of confidence, arrogance, betraying trust, or immoral/unethical lifestyles.

*Discussion Questions*

1. Take a closer look at Dr. Ridley's list of 13 factors. List them in order from the one in which you would score the highest to the lowest. How can you begin working on the lowest three factors on your list?
2. Describe a time when you have exhibited confidence. What makes confidence possible?
3. What does your confidence say about your relationship with God?
4. Why is it hard for people in leadership to admit their mistakes?
5. Which of these potential threats—lack of confidence, arrogance, betraying trust, or immoral/unethical lifestyles—has the greatest potential to undermine your leadership? What can you do to strengthen yourself in this area of vulnerability?

*Next Steps*

1. Identify one or more of the 13 factors on which you need to work.
2. Ask a mentor to help you develop a strategy for improving your confidence.
3. Make increasing the amount of time you spend with God in His Word a priority.
4. Identify one leadership mistake and discuss it with a trusted friend.
5. Review the list of potential threats and develop a plan to strengthen yourself in any weak areas.

# CHAPTER 5

# BE MEAN ABOUT THE VISION

*"You will kill the vision God gave you for the church if you spend your resources on pieces that don't feed into the overall vision."*

Vision.

Let me be honest, the very mention of the word sends shivers down my spine. Not because I am scared of vision or casting it, but it reminds me of CONFERENCES! Every generation has their mark on Christendom, and the Baby Boomers injected the conference into the mix.

Oh yes, vision. Back to the point.

I don't have the expertise, nor am I enough of a leadership guru to elaborately maneuver you through creating a vision and then help you cast one. Andy Stanley is the man to learn from; look his stuff up.

There are plenty of books out there that deal with this subject head on. In fact, I even found blogs when I searched this subject that reject the idea that a church should have a vision and mission. They suggested it is ungodly. Oh, please!

Vision—simply defined—is the course, path, direction your Jesus community is taking and who you will be along the way.

A pastor in a nearby city from us used to say that the church's mission statement was the Great Commission and that we didn't need anything else. I agree to a point, but HOW will we fulfill the Great Commission? I haven't met a church that didn't believe their job was to fulfill the Great Commission. For the church this pastor was overseeing, it was an attractional community that really saw themselves as a voice in the community.

Going back to our discussion on mindsets of the church, they were of the PROPHET mindset. So, if someone came to the church that had a mindset that the church was to fulfill the Great Commission by acts of service, how would this be communicated to this new church member?

Does it just remain unsaid that this is who the church is?
Because that is exactly how most of our churches act.

It is important to be able to answer the question of who your community is, where it is going, and how it is going to get there.

When we first began working on Elevation Church, Ryan and I came up with words that described who we were and what we wanted the community of followers of Jesus to develop as their culture.

It would always catch me off guard when someone asked us to state our church-plant's mission. I would stumble through my words trying to come up with something that put all the pieces together. It was there inside of us, but we had never formally put it down on paper and processed what it looked like.

It is about disciples.
Got it.
Check.
How will we do that?
What is our mindset?

Who are we? Because you will attract who you are. And by attract, I am not talking just about who shows up to a service, but the relationships you will build and form along the journey.

I encourage you to process this. Church-planting boot camps and preps will walk you through this process. Pick up a book on vision from Jedi Masters Andy Stanley or John Maxwell. (Apparently living in Atlanta gives you the ability to be an amazing leader.)

So—after you know who you are,
where you are going,
can see down the road,
know what your Jesus community is going to be and how they are going to do it . . .

What next?

No one ever told me this, but when a new church opens in any city in America, a snowstorm occurs. Every flake shows up. I don't know how they know it, but you will get the craziest people at the very beginning.

With the new relationships you are naturally building, with the type of ministry outreach you are doing, with the public gatherings and service, people will want to be part of your new church community and will not know your vision. Most likely, they will have their own vision for how the church should operate too.

The hijackers will come.
They will come to hijack the vision that God has birthed in you for this new Jesus community.
Be MEAN about the VISION.

Don't let anyone hijack the mission and vision of the church.
If God wanted it done a different way, He would have told you.

Your job is not to make other followers of Jesus happy with your new Jesus community. Your job is to build new relationships with people who don't know Jesus and disciple them into spiritual maturity. Those who don't know Jesus yet will almost never come with preconceived ideas of what a church vision should be or how it should be done.

Be MEAN about the VISION.
Don't let Christians show up and take over the church community.

Every church planter experiences this, but for some reason it is almost never talked about. I am telling you right now that a day will come in the life of your church-plant when someone will either come to you directly or will begin to try to steer the vision of the church community in a way that is contrary to what God has told you and your team.

No apologies.
Be MEAN about the VISION.

Looking back at the infancy of Elevation Church, I can count three to four people who we had to directly deal with as they tried to hijack the vision. We did our best to make sure that we communicated very publicly who we were, and we did things to drive away those who might try to join the hijacking ranks.

In the early stages of the church, one guy who started attending Elevation with his family stated, "We are looking for a church to serve." The first red flag should have gone up immediately, because the true translation of those words are, "We want to be in leadership, do you want us to lead?"

The guy had a wealth of past experiences, none that we could really substantiate. As our team began to get to know this guy, he would constantly start discussions about the new church-plant with statements like,

"I believe church should be like this . . ."
"YOU do church differently than I've seen."
"YOU have to do it this way . . ."

KEY OBSERVATION: If someone is part of your community and they refer to it as "you" or "you guys," then they really are not part of the community. They view themselves as an outsider. This is what we were experiencing with this guy.

He came to me with ideas of a how he could run a non-profit that Elevation would form. I had received similar proposals from other members. I did think he had a cool idea, but I just couldn't see it when I spent time praying to God. This guy wouldn't stop, though. He would hound me with how we were not following God because of the way we were doing ministry. I didn't want to do it, because I value relationships, but I had to get this guy out of our community. He was just toxic to the vision.

Be MEAN about the VISION.
Protect it.

## Potential Church-Plant Hijackers

You need to be aware of eight different types of people that will show up to your church and hijack the vision if you don't take action immediately.

### The Fixer

Fixers will come in feeling that God has called them to repair something about you and the church. They will use language like "you" when referring to the church and will tell you constantly how to do ministry. They will have a history of attending several churches and never being committed to one church. They will consider themselves experts; sometimes they will have advanced degrees in religion and even pastoral credentials. They have no fruit from past ministry, just a lot of theory to share with you.

They are generally condescending in their speech. It is hard for them to build deep relationships and usually will bend on the more legalistic side of things.

A good warning sign of who these people are is if you can't find any substantially deep relationships in their lives with those they were in ministry during the past. Fixers try to fix everyone and don't ever build deep relationships.

We had one such "fixer" in our church a few years back. He was leading a house church for us. One of my worst mistakes as a leader. I knew this guy was trouble, but he had the credentials, and I needed a leader for this one particular house church.

One night my doorbell rang. Standing on the other side of my door was a couple from the church who got saved our very first month of public gatherings. My co-pastor Ryan had even bought the husband his first Bible for Christmas. This couple was a blessing from God and fruit of the new Jesus community. They lived almost thirty minutes away from my house, and it was late.

This was an unusual visit.
I could see it in their eyes. Something was wrong.

"Come in."

"We need to talk to you, Trinity."

They made their way to my couch and sat down. The wife couldn't look me in the eyes. This was not going to be a good conversation.

"If you don't get rid of our house church leader, and if he stays in our church, we are going to leave. We don't feel like this guy is healthy for us, for you, the church, and where God is taking us."

I wasn't shocked. I could have guessed this would happen. "What has been going on at the house church that brings you to this conclusion?"

"He is trying to fix all of us! He taught the whole house church not to go to Vegas and gamble, ridiculed us for playing poker, told us that allowing our kids to dress up for Halloween is demonic, and then told all of the couples in the house church that the only biblical way to have sex was the missionary position!"

My thoughts immediately went to thinking about everyone who was in that house church. There was a lady in her sixties in who attended without her husband. I could only imagine what she thought about the sex teaching, how embarrassing it would have been to be in that house church. It was a surprise that I didn't have the whole house church outside my door that night.

I understood some of this guy's teaching, but some of it was crazy. His methods appeared to be killing the people in this group.

That night I made a promise and followed through, that I would remove the house church leader and have a long talk with him about who we were in church community and who we were not. I could see that a lot of his teachings in the house church were preferences, but I knew that it stemmed from a much bigger issue of this guy being a fixer.

He left the church shortly after we removed him from leading a house church. My regret is that I didn't respond earlier to the flags I saw and walk a little more observantly through his involvement in our community.

### Mr. Tunnel Visioner

The tunnel visioners are not bad people. They are usually very passionate and work really hard at what they love.

The problem is that they have this ONE thing that they think everyone should be involved with and care about. They think that if everyone worshiped for twenty-four hours a day and fasted three days a week, then the ills of the world would be broken. They might have their favorite service project or nonprofit that they are involved with and want others to be involved with them. They will want to add whatever is their passion to the church, and if it isn't there they will leave or pout like a little kid.

This was the case for the story I told you earlier about the guy and his proposal to Elevation Church. You will get proposals from people in your church who will be so passionate about the project or ministry. Does the vision encompass this strategy they are proposing? If it doesn't, be MEAN about the VISION.

Tunnel visioners will drain resources from your church if you let them. They will get people going in a different direction and hijack the vision by sucking the energy in a whole different direction. Tunnel visioners will create a cancerous tumor on the church that, if left to itself, will eventually kill the church community by changing it from what it was designed to do.

Now, I am not talking about someone who is passionate about an area of ministry you guys are doing as a church, like kids ministry, but even someone can get so tunnel visioned in an area of ministry it can hurt the big-picture vision of the church.

### Mr. Romantic
You will see a lot of romantics throughout the life of your church.

The romantics are those who will fantasize about how church should be and how your church doesn't add up. Specifically, their fantasies will stem from their "last church." Any talk of their last church will seem as though the pastor was Jesus Christ in the flesh. They will start a lot of their statements with, "My last church . . ." or "My former church . . ." or "My home church . . ." or "My church back home . . ."

The romantics are really good people. They are just caught up in either the ideal of what they could see a church being or doing, OR they had such a great church experience with their last church, nothing will ever compare.

Romantics can be tough to get to "buy in" to the vision of your new church community. It is like dating someone who was once married and can't believe they are not with their spouse anymore. You will be compared to everything that the former spouse ever did or didn't do. Their heart isn't really with you, and lots of healing needs to take place for them to realize the present reality they find themselves in. Romantics are in love with something that doesn't exist.

Until a romantic can give up the fantasy of what church is or isn't and be part of the community with their whole heart, they will just cause frustration and dissent to the vision. Their dissent isn't an attacking negative dissent. It is usually spoken through kind words and smiles, but its roots are infectiously negative thoughts about the approach you will be taking with the church-plant.

One such romantic attended Elevation Church. She was such a great lady. Yet, everything we did I had to hear those famous words, "At my last church we . . ." If we decided to do a block party, I had to hear about how awesome her last church did a block party and how we should do it. Eventually, I sat her down and looked her in the eyes and said, "This is not your last church. We will never be your last church. You will never find a church that is exactly like your last church. You will find similarities but nothing exact. We or any other church will never be *yours* until you admit you are not part of your last church anymore. You allowing us to be your church and do things differently doesn't mean that your last church is any less of a church than us, because they are different from us. You loving us as your new church isn't us replacing the church community you once belonged to, it is us being part of a different time in your life."

We also had a gentleman who loved us so much and was so involved, but everything we did we had to hear about how the early church fathers would have done it. And how if everyone who was following Jesus in our church would just do x, y, or z, we would be this or that. He had such a deep love for what the church could be that he never saw what we were and how we were growing in maturity. His love was a fantasy of where we were going instead of who we were.

I snapped one day when he was talking to me about how so many of our new followers of Jesus didn't know the Bible and if they did what we would be. I told him "I know your desire is for everyone to grow in their maturity in Christ. If you always compare them to what they should be and not love them for who they are, they will never want to listen to a thing you have to say. I don't even like listening to you. Love them for who they are, and see them for what they can be."

## Mr. Negative

I almost don't need to explain this one. We all know who this guy is. Nothing is ever right, done right, taught right, or good in their eyes. They never have a nice thing to say about the church, but for some reason they are at every event your church has. They are involved, they serve, they give, but they just suck the life right out of you with their negative words and demeanor. Eventually, you just hate being around them. It's as if your soul seeps from you when they are around. They almost seem to have forgotten how to smile in life or know the word "laugh." Negative people are really some of the most dangerous people to have in your church.

Let me clarify something: Sometimes people are so hurt and broken that they seem to pour all that negative spirit out on those around them. These people usually are not complainers of the church community at large. They are just very wounded people and need lots of love and grace.

I am talking more about the people that seem to have the spiritual gift of negative criticism. They like to send you e-mails telling you why something is wrong. Every time they get a chance to talk to you it is about a problem. You can't remember a time that they were actually leading others to Jesus or serving with a smile on their face.

Get rid of them ASAP.

They will stall out the execution of the vision faster than almost anyone. They will undermine the authority of leaders, and if they sense you are not taking them seriously, they will go behind your back and speak ill of your leadership decisions to everyone. They derail the confidence of the community. Gossip is their weapon.

These people are toxic.

When you spot them, you need to confront them. If they keep up with the negative verbiage, you need to ask them to leave. Your young church doesn't need to have such an infectious disease at such an early stage.

We haven't had too many Mr. Negatives in the life of our young church. Usually because I spot them pretty fast. We had a major one when we first started. One of our leaders, who is never negative, would always come to leadership meetings sharing negative talk that someone had told him in confidence. We talked to our staff member on how to deal with this person, but finally we had to simply remove that Mr. Negative from being involved in anything. He left without us having to ask him to. Almost immediately we saw a change in the spirit of the people in the community that this person used to influence.

## Mr. Anti-Church

Anti-church has been reading too many Brian McLaren and Frank Viola books. They have this view that the church is wrong in how it is structured, how it operates, and that all is wrong with modern-day evangelical churches.

I agree that much is wrong—just not all of it.

The generalization that these anti-church people lay on each church doesn't allow for them to be part of the solution; it just keeps us debating instead of doing. They don't believe in authority and submission—even to the Word of God—and no one in their life can tell them "no."

I am always curious why these anti-church people show up in churches. If their deep beliefs and thoughts on church led them to be anti-church, why do they participate in something they don't agree with? I guess it's because deep down, everyone has a desire for acceptance in our lives and wanting to be around people.

My experience with this anti-church crowd has shown me that they usually have great hearts to serve and minister, but they will not commit, submit, give financially, and will not go along with the vision. Some of them can be very vocal, but the ones I have dealt with are low-key on their vocalized thoughts. They usually express themselves in smaller settings when no leaders are present.

I heard Mark Driscoll describe people in the church by using animals as his descriptions. He used the cow to describe the people in your church that eat up all your resources but do no real work. The anti-church crowd is close. They eat up all your resources and will only give when they feel it fits with their personal theological stance. They are the only authority in their life. We attract a bunch of these types. I am sure we could process that and figure out why, but we are pretty good at handling them. We love them, but we don't let them get anywhere close to being the influencers.

We designed a ten-week class called *Joining the Journey* in which we go over our DNA, our biblical beliefs, and what we expect of those who call themselves followers of Jesus and are part of our Jesus community. We require that if you are going to serve in any leadership position, you must take this class.

The anti-church crowd will not submit their time for ten weeks, so it gets rid of them from leadership positions real fast.

One such person who used to attend our church met with me for lunch. He scheduled the meeting, so I was curious to what he wanted to talk about. He went on to tell me about how he felt that a church should never have a building and how unbiblical it was. His last church had started a building campaign, so he left. He liked that we gave to nonprofits in the area that were curing social injustice but didn't see any biblical evidence for me as the pastor making the decisions with our elders on how we were to spend the money. He also didn't think we should take up offerings.

I asked him, "How could we pay for the rental of the locations we meet in? How could we support these nonprofits that you feel are doing biblical things? Is there biblical evidence for them asking for money? This is who we are, and this is what we have chosen to do in following Jesus. It might not be perfect, but we don't think we are sinning in how we operate. If you can't get behind that, then you need to find a place where you can."

He stuck around for almost another year. He liked the teachings on Sundays and the worship experience, but eventually he stopped going to church altogether.

Anti-church people will never submit to the influence of the leaders because they are poisoned with distrust and an independent spirit. In many ways, God has made us co-dependent on each other as we follow Jesus.

Keep your eyes on the anti-church crowd. Some may need to be gently pushed out; others just need you to be very direct with them about who you are and who you are not. Don't let them put a negative umbrella over the vision.

**Mr. Jack Russell Terrier**

I can handle all the other types of vision derailers I have mentioned so far, but the Jack Russell Terrier drives me bananas. I avoid them when I see 'em coming.

The Jack Russell Terriers have lots of energy, lots of passion, but they just make a lot of noise and have no attention span. They can't focus on anything in the church; they live in their own little world of thoughts and excitement. When they answer a question in a small group, they don't answer the question but run to some thought in their head they just want to express to the rest of the group. They usually read other church leaders' blogs, listen to other podcasts, and read lots of books. They are inspired and excited easily. You can't get them to settle down or focus on one thing.

They are loving.
They are servers.
They are givers.
They are actively part of your Jesus community.

Yet they almost just don't get it.
They don't settle down on one thing and work at that one thing for the bigger vision.

Jack Russell Terriers don't fit in and will show up at your new church because they just didn't fit in at their last church. They are the "extra grace required" types. My heart goes out to them. They seem to live in this insanity of jumping around from thing to thing, thought to thought, excitement to excitement—but they don't get anything done.

Keep Jack Russell Terriers away from leadership!

They will frustrate those who they are leading and will never actually lead people anywhere. Give them small service jobs and let them do those one at a time. Throw the ball in one direction, and when they bring it back, give them a new assignment.

**Mr. Supporter**
We talked earlier about those who have tunnel vision and those who are romantics.

Sometimes you will come across people who will have a passion for a ministry and fantasy for how things should be. You will see the confidence in their eyes. You will see the passion in their soul. You will see the natural leadership and influence that radiates from them.

If what they are passionate about and have a vision for doesn't fit with the church, don't do it. You will have a tendency to bend the vision to accommodate these people. They are really great people and great leaders.

They submit.
They are bought in.

They want to merge what they are doing into the vision of the church. It doesn't fit. You don't want them to leave and go somewhere else.

Don't miss this: Being MEAN about the VISION also entails not inserting pieces into that vision that don't fit. If it doesn't fit, it doesn't fit. You can't force a puzzle piece into the wrong puzzle.

They might be shiny. The leader might be sharp. The idea of having their passion and ministry attached to your church community is tempting.

You need to support their passion and vision. They need to not be part of what you are doing. They need to go and do their own thing. They need to find a place that fits with what they want to do, and you can be their supporter.

These will be the hardest people to recognize.

You will be tempted to integrate every single great leader's idea and passion into the overall vision. You will kill the vision God gave you for the church if you spend your resources on pieces that don't feed into the overall vision. If you attached pieces, they will eventually need to be removed to save the health of the vision. Just don't attach them.

I love how Rick Warren is now focusing the next twenty years on things outside the walls of Saddleback, specifically church planting. The first twenty years was about the ministry within its walls, but now it is on the world around them. Rick was always supportive of those who wanted to plant churches, but it wasn't part of the vision of Saddleback. They didn't add it until it was part of the vision.

We have such a great guy in our church who has an amazing heart and passion for doing a very specific ministry in a city that is almost thirty miles from one of our campuses. He has an amazing strategy and support for what he is doing, but it doesn't fit with the overall vision of our Jesus community. The best thing we could do for him and us was to support him the best way we can to help him get his own ministry going. We help him with accounting and administration work right now. Maybe one day our vision will expand, but right now it would hurt him and us.

Lots of relationships get ruined because a pastor can't be honest with someone and tell them that they don't see something fitting with the church. The pastor keeps them strung along because they don't want to lose them. They are NOT ours to lose. They are God's.

God has put these passions inside of them, and we need to help them be who God created them to be without killing the vision of the church.

I am sure there are other types of people we can identify who have the tendency to hijack the vision of the church, but these are the most common. You will need God's discernment in dealing with each one of them. Treat them as individuals, not as a category. I categorized them here for teaching purposes, not for your interaction with them. Remember everyone's past—the good, bad, ugly is all why they are who they are. Treat them with respect, but be firm.

Don't use the typical pastor talk where you don't say what you really mean.

You will notice in these categories that all of these people have past church experience. I have yet to have someone who came to know Jesus in our church community try to derail the vision. They are bought in more than anyone. It is always those who come from other churches that we have to watch out for. Not that everyone with church experience is a derailer. It is the one thing that all derailers seem to have in common.

Best way to make sure that people don't hijack the vision is to do what you were commanded to do. Make disciples. If you are helping other people to start a relationship with Jesus and teaching them all that He has for them, then you will not be spending your time recruiting people from other churches.

Be MEAN about the VISION.
Protect it at all costs.

# Chapter Five in Review

*Key Ideas*

1. Vision is foundational to your present and future ministry.
2. Church planters must be able to define their community and express vision for its future development.
3. Without a clearly articulated vision, others will take a church where it never intended to go.
4. Different types of people will show up and try to hijack your vision for the church.
5. The best defense against vision drift is a commitment to making disciples.

*Discussion Questions*

1. Why is it important that you have a vision for your new church?
2. How would you describe your faith community? Who are they and where do you want to take them?
3. Review the different kinds of people who will show up in your church. Which ones have you ignored and what have been the consequences?
4. Why is it so important that the vision for your church be protected at all costs?
5. What are three things you can do to begin making disciples?

*Next Steps*

1. Evaluate your vision statement and adjust it as needed.
2. Draw a circle representing the description of your community. Who is inside the circle? Who is outside? Is there a ministry targeting those who are outside your circle?

3. Identify the potential problem-people within your community and make plans to spend one-on-one time with each of them.

4. Create a communications strategy regarding your vision.

5. Speak with an educational professional about your discipleship strategy.

# CHAPTER 6

# THERE IS NO "I" IN TEAM ... WELL, UNLESS APPLE GETS AHOLD OF IT

*"If your focus is only about your public gatherings in recruiting team members, they will never share in the PURPOSE that God has called you to."*

Hindsight is always twenty-twenty.

If only I could go back and do things differently. What pain could I have avoided? Could we have made a bigger impact? Would more people be following Jesus?

I don't let the questions of "what if" keep me down, but I want to help you learn from my journey.

One of those areas that I felt we did a so-so job was in the area of building a team.

My wife and I moved to the area where the new church-plant would be located the same day that our co-pastor and his family moved into the area as well. We both arrived on the same day to our community to begin building relationships.

It started with two families with a shared vision.

We knew we needed others to join our "core" long before we could see the multiplication process take off. It was about addition in the beginning, and it will be for you as well.

God may have planted the seed of a new Jesus community in your heart and mind, but He uses PEOPLE (plural) to accomplish His purposes. The kingdom of God is not an individual or spectator sport. God builds it through His people.

We went to the trainings our church-planting network wanted us to attend. One of the segments was on getting team members.

What I noticed, looking back, was that the team teaching was about recruiting people to do your Sunday services. BUT it isn't about services! It is about discipleship. If your focus is only about your public gatherings in recruiting team members, they will never share in the PURPOSE that God has called you to.

We left the training and started to think what type of people we needed to join us. Our decision was to recruit people who FIT with us.

Who had our mindset?

We also decided that we wanted people who didn't have experience working in a church. No preconceived ideas of how things were to be done, and we could be the ones to mold their minds to the purpose of church.

Our first recruit was a twenty-something young lady who had been in my youth ministry in the past. She was part of a discipleship team in Texas and had a heart to see kids come to Jesus. Since we were living in the youngest state in the U.S. and we were in the youngest-per-capita area in the U.S. at the time, we felt that having someone with her heart and passion was a plus.

Our next recruit was a guy right out of high school from Colorado who looked like Napoleon Dynamite (or as he says, Napoleon Dynamite looks like him). Through personal connections with this guy, I knew he thought of church as different from what we had all experienced, and he was into communicating through video and graphics.

The next person to join our team came the way that church planting should bring people: through discipleship. A guy I had met at a family party in Utah began to engage me in Jesus questions.

He called me one day, "Hey Trinity, can you go to the movies with me?"

"Sorry bud, I'm already married, but thanks for the offer. I am flattered."

"No, No. My wife and I want to go to a movie with you and your wife. We know we are going to have questions, and we think you are the only one to answer them."

"Cool. My wife and I would love to hang with you guys. What movie are we seeing?"

"It is called *The Passion of the Christ*. Have you heard of it?"

Had I heard of it? What evangelical in the U.S. hadn't heard of it or bought out a theater to bring every person they knew to it? Every evangelical I knew thought the movie was going to save the world. Of course I had heard of it.

"Yep, I've heard of it."

"Have you seen it already?"

He had no clue that I had seen it like three times. Not only did I think it was a great film, but my former church had done outreaches with buying out every seat in the theaters.

"Well, I've seen it, but I would love to see it again with you."

We set the time, date, and off we went. After the movie we went to Olive Garden to chat about the film. "Trinity, why is this story so important?"

"I'm glad you asked." I went on to share my story of redemption and salvation. My wife followed up with her story of grace and love. I gave him a Bible on CD for him to listen to on his long commutes to work and told him we should talk after he listens to each book.

The next week I get a call. "Trinity, I just listened to Matthew. It was exactly like the movie we watched."

"Yep."

Next day.
"Trinity, I just listened to Mark. Man, it is a lot like Matthew."

"Well, you will be shocked on the next one."

The next day.
"Finished Luke and John. Finally glad that John said something different. I was beginning to think every book was the story of the movie we watched."

The next day.
"I just finished Galatians, and I get it! Rules can't make you a good person, it is only through Jesus."

We started our first house church because of his conversion. He was so on fire to share his newfound belief with everyone, and we were seeing major changes in this guy's spiritual life. It was contagious to our core group.

Okay, this is why I said we did a so-so job. We started with a solid team. Two families, two single core team members, and one on-fire, brand-new disciple.

Slowly, through our house church and discipleship, we gained more and more families. The families were awesome, but they were not really team members.

If I could go back, I would have spent more time and energy recruiting more people to be part of our team from the beginning. We had great people, but there wasn't enough of us to fulfill the vision God had given us. It was like putting together a football team and only having four really good players and one guy who was brand new to the game. Five of us were never going to be able to do it all.

Scott Bruegman, a church planter in Denver, did things a little different. He spent a few years living in the community he wanted to plant a church, recruiting team members to share in the vision, and raising the financial resources to see the vision through. The Jesus community that was birthed out of Scott's efforts was a success on many levels—the biggest one in my book being that people came to know Jesus and began a discipleship journey.

We jumped into DOING the outreach a lot faster than we should have. More time was needed in putting a solid team together. We were running plays long before a playbook was designed. Now that I know that, I love helping other planters identify what they need in their launch team.

A team will accelerate the ultimate outcome of your vision.
A team will make light the burden you will carry. Many hands make light work.
A team will support you when you are down. Not everyone can have a bad day at once.
A team will pray together and for each other. Spiritual insight from others is important.

Over the years, I have seen how our core team reflects everything we are as a Jesus community. One person cannot be the reflection of community. Those who are not following Jesus see our devotion to one another and want that in their life, and those who are following Jesus see something modeled for them as an example.

Teams are important.

There is no I in TEAM.

You can't make this about you.

If you do, it will die by you as well.

What happens when you leave?
What happens when something happens to you?

A team makes it possible for the legacy and life of the church to live long beyond one person's personality and charisma.

I'm sure this is why we see plurality all over the pages of Scripture:

We always think of Moses as going at it alone. He wasn't alone, God sent him Aaron.
Moses' father-in-law convinced Moses he couldn't govern by himself.
Jesus sent His followers out in groups of two, never alone.
Jesus Himself worked in a team of 12, and an inner team of 3.
Paul went out in teams with John Mark, Barnabas, Luke, and later

Timothy. Paul writes to both Timothy and Titus to put together teams to lead the church.

Could it be any wonder why our God is three in one?

It is never about one person. You are more likely to die on the vine if you do this on your own. God didn't design it that way, and your first step in putting flesh to the vision is to recruit a team.

What to look for in core team members as you recruit . . .

### Trust

Paul starts off talking to Timothy in chapter 3 of his first letter to him about character issues in those who he recruits to be leaders. If people's character is intact, they are easy to trust. You need to be able to trust them, and you need them to be someone whom others trust.

Paul says these are the character traits that your team members need to have:

- Living above the level of accusations
- Not saying one thing, doing another, or saying one thing here and another there
- Not looking to get more and more and more
- Not letting anything control them in life other than Jesus
- Good reputation by those who know them
- Not in love with money
- Not one who likes to start fights and arguments

- Gentle
- Not a drunk
- Welcoming of others
- Worthy of respect
- Self-disciplined and controlled
- Clearly focused on what is right and good

If I could add to his list of character traits, I would add two:
- Not a gossip
- Loyal to a fault

The best way to discover these character qualities in someone is to ask lots of deep, personal questions that relate to each one of these areas. Then get references from those who are closest to the person and ask them similar questions. Finding previous church communities that they were part of and talking to the leaders there is always a huge help. You don't want to get caught off guard down the road.

Trust is about knowing what the other person is going to do in a situation and feeling comfortable with their actions. If you put people on your team who you are suspicious of and you don't trust, you will turn your fluid team into a hiccup.

If you can find these qualities in someone, you can speed up the trust process if they are new to your life. It's easy to grab people we have known over time and feel comfortable with to join us, only to find out that there is a character flaw we didn't know of so we end up losing trust in them along the journey. Trust is more than knowing someone. Trust comes with knowledge and character.

The young lady we recruited at the very beginning began to show us character flaws along the way. I took the fact that I had known her for so long as a basis for trust on our team. We realized that we couldn't trust her any longer on our team. She, too, could see her own character flaws when we talked to her about them so she withdrew from our team immediately.

Your team members need your trust. You need their trust. You have to know that they have your back in this journey.

A good book to read is *The Speed of Trust* by Stephen Covey. You will enjoy the insight he has in learning to trust those you work with.

### Fit

Jim Collins will probably forever be known as the guy who put the analogy of "getting the right people on the bus" from his book *Good to Great*. Not only do you need to trust your team members, but they really have to fit with the whole puzzle. Everything from the vision, to the other team members, to the environment they will be working in, and how their family fits with the culture of the new Jesus community.

You want diversity on the team.

Paul talks about how different the body of Christ is when he writes to the church in Corinth. You can't have six hands and no legs. Diversity is good, and you should seek out diversity on the team. One way that we do this now is by giving all of our recruits a personality test to see who they are and how they compare with the rest of us. We want to have balance and wholeness to our team, and that only comes from diversity.

Even though you want diversity, you want each of your team members to have working chemistry. You might really hit it off with someone you are recruiting and find that you can trust them and connect with them. What if the rest of the team can't connect? You don't need that unnecessary friction in the new community you are working to create. Your previously recruited team members should get a say in bringing on board the next team members in relation to chemistry.

I know I have a different philosophy of the church leadership team strategy than some pastors, so you might not agree with me here. I believe each team member of mine must have chemistry with me that goes beyond just being able to work together. I don't want anyone on my team who I wouldn't be willing to vacation with in life. You don't vacation with people you dislike (okay, maybe in-laws . . . but besides them). Mark Batterson shared this thought with me, and I have kept it as a personal value in my team. (The thought about wanting to vacation with your staff, not the in-laws.)

Remember, it is easier to add someone to the team than it is to remove him.

Make sure they fit.
Make sure they know what they are getting into.
Make sure the rest of the team approves of the new team member.

Make sure that their family is a fit.

We had one couple that came to join our team. Great couple. They joined about two years into the church-planting process. We found as time went on that one of them just didn't fit with the rest of the team and the church community. It wasn't that something was wrong with that person; it was just a matter of chemistry. I could tell it was making that individual miserable, and it was putting stress on our whole team and volunteer workers. We had to let them go but were happy to help them find another church-planting team that we supported and felt they did fit with. They are really blossoming in their new community, which makes everyone happy.

Don't force a puzzle piece into the puzzle if it doesn't fit.

### Competency

Do your potential team members have the competency to do what you expect of them on the team?

Maybe you find someone who loves to communicate visually. They want to do graphics and video for the new community. You trust them. They have the most outstanding character. They may fit you like a glove. BUT their graphics and video work is terrible or they have no clue how to use a computer to do graphics. Well, then you probably don't want them to be on the team to communicate visually.

Competency is more than having the knowledge to do a particular task, but understanding the bigger vision. You want someone who understands why their service in a particular area is so crucial to the overall goal and destination of the rest of the community.

For us, we don't want anyone on our team who doesn't understand that it is all about leading people to Jesus and discipling them. Everything we do, from preaching, house churches, kids ministry, to youth ministry, has one goal: discipleship. We want to take ourselves and others deeper. We need team members who understand this and are able to take their areas of leadership and mold them to help us reach that end.

You will find a lot of people willing to help you out, but you need to recruit competent LEADERS at the beginning:

Leaders are able to organize, recruit, and delegate responsibility to workers.
Leaders are able to build smaller teams beyond the team you are recruiting.

Workers are doers. They complete tasks. If you want to micro-manage and have your hands in every relationship in the new Jesus community, then recruit workers.

If you want to see multiplication take place after you add your core team, then recruit LEADERS.

I know a lot has been written lately on deciding whom to pay in the beginning stages of your church-plant. A lot of thoughts have been thrown out there. You probably can name a dozen without much effort. Here are some suggestions I encountered regularly when I was just starting:

- Stipend all positions that you would want to see as a full-time position if the ministry grew.
- Pay those you can't afford to lose.
- Stipend those who you need to organizationally control.
- Pay those who are the top leaders.

Let me suggest a different approach. I think we have professionalized the church too much and have taken away from what Paul told the church in Ephesus about the work of the leaders in the church. We were given to the church to build up the ministry by training and equipping the church community to do the work of the ministry. When we pay people to do the work of the ministry, we take it out of the hands of who the church IS. If you pull your ministry workers out of the world and put them in a church building and pay them to work, you—in essence—pull them from the very place where they are supposed to be doing MINISTRY!

Pay those who produce leadership, training and equipping the church community to do the work of the ministry. Don't pay those who do ministry.

Pay those who are your LEADERS, building the teams. Don't pay those who are on the teams.

## Buy-In

Recruit core team members who are bought in. They have to WANT to do this. You don't want someone who thinks your church-plant is a "good idea." When the tough days come (and they will), you want them to stand with you, even if it all goes bad.

Put people on that core team who will bleed with you.
They need to have caught the vision and are ready to sell out for it.

I knew that when Ryan, my co-pastor, heard the vision I had and when I heard the vision he had, they were the same. We were both willing to do anything we could to see it happen. In fact, both of us bought houses in an area with no jobs and no guarantee of success. We believed what God had asked of us and shown us. We were in.

If you have to talk people into being on the team, why would you want them there? Someone else will come along and talk them into leaving one day.

I watch too much sports on TV. I pay attention to all of the chatter on programs whether they focus on professional or collegiate sports. Just the other day an NCAA football coach was discussing how his players were giving up scholarships from other schools to walk on to his football team, which means they are paying for school on their own and don't really have a roster spot on the team.

The interview was so interesting because after he was describing this, a former NFL player who was also in studio for the interview said this: "A culture has been created where everyone there wants to play, is hungry to compete, and is bought into the vision of this football program."

The coach then said something like, "Why would I ever try to convince anyone to play for me? If I have to convince them, then I will struggle with getting them to listen to me when I coach them to do something different from what they are used to doing. I want them to trust me and want them to do what I say. That starts with being on the team."

I have two guys on our team right now who have been offered two to three times their pay to go work at other churches. I love it when I get e-mails from other leaders asking me if they can talk to my team members about joining their team. I always say yes because . . .

. . . I don't want to stand in the way of something God might be doing in their life or ours.
. . . If they are not bought in to what we are doing, then they should probably go find a different place to minister.

Every time these churches ask these two guys on our team, they are told no without hesitation. It is not about the money or the opportunity that exists somewhere else. It is about the vision God has spoken to them.

You need team members who have that conviction about the vision.

You need team members who are willing to do whatever it takes to get the job done. If it means we need to get an elephant into an Apple store to lead people to Jesus, then your team members should start working to see how to get it done. (I just thought of the most outrageous thing I could; please don't put an elephant in an Apple store.)

Your team will be the second level of your foundation in this new Jesus community. The first level is Jesus, and we know He is solid. Put a solid team on top of that to equip Jesus' followers to do the ministry. If you do this and spend the time doing it right, you will have lots of success.

# Chapter Six in Review

*Key Ideas*

1. Church planting is a team sport.
2. Church planters must recruit people who fit their strategy and vision.
3. The effectiveness of a church-plant is directly related to its focus on moving people into authentic community. Small groups are more vital than large gatherings.
4. Leadership teams accelerate the implementation of your vision.
5. Not everyone who comes in should be given a leadership role.

*Discussion Questions*

1. What are the key leadership roles necessary for your church-plant to begin?
2. What questions should you ask to determine if people are supportive of your strategy and vision?
3. Why is it so important that the church be built upon the foundation of small discipleship and leadership teams?
4. How can leadership teams accelerate your church's establishment?
5. What characteristics are you looking for in leaders? Which leadership positions do you see as future staff positions?

*Next Steps*

1. Define the key leadership roles necessary to implement your vision.
2. Make a list of questions you will ask every potential leader.

3. Speak with a small groups professional about the process for starting small groups in conjunction with your church-plant.
4. Define the leadership teams you believe will be critical to your work.
5. List the qualities expected in leaders and ask all potential leaders to evaluate themselves in each area.

# CHAPTER 7

# HARDEST DUDE TO RECRUIT
# WILL BE BENJAMIN

*"People will invest their money and prayers in those they believe in, but they will never give when feeling sold to."*

As soon as we received approval from our church planting organization to start a new church, we knew we were going to need the Benjamins to pull off making the vision a reality. We did what we had seen everyone else do when asking for money in the church world.

We wrote a really nice letter.

Plus, we put together a great packet of information. Brainstormed every name and address of potential givers. In the end, we sent out four hundred packets and letters. Our letters included a pledge form and an envelope for them to start supporting us right away.

We really didn't have a budget in mind, nor did we have a goal. We figured that out of four hundred potential giving units, at least one hundred units would give. We prayed that those one hundred would give big or on a monthly basis so that we would have enough money to figure out how to make the vision a reality.

Two envelopes came back.

My mom gave. And another family member gave generously. That's it.

I was destroyed inside. This vision was from God, so surely the resources were supposed to follow the vision, right?

You can have an amazing vision. You could have had a personal visit from Mother Mary, Jesus, and the president of the United States. You could "know that you know" that God has called you to plant a church, but unless you work at finding the funds and financial resources to launch that vision, you will be left with just a vision.

God has a way of partnering with us. God works out the redemption and salvation of the world, but He does it through people.

John Wesley once said, "Pray like it depends on God, work like it depends on you."

In the same way you will be formulating strategy, finding team members, developing disciples, and building relationships. YOU will depend on the help and work of God to intervene. Nothing happens without the work of the Holy Spirit in our lives.

The same is true for finances. Without God, we'll spend a lot of time kicking up dust with very little to show for it.

Let's talk about what is good work toward attaining financial resources and what is not good work.

The first step in all of this is figuring out a budget for your new church-plant. We didn't do this at all. Thankfully, our missions organization that oversees U.S. endeavors approved us after we had sent out four hundred letters, put us through proper training, and developed a personal and work budget for us. Most missions and church planting organizations will help you develop a budget.

Divide this up by stages.
*Stage 1: Pre-Launch*
*Stage 2: Pre-Launch // Ministry*
*Stage 3: Launch // Infancy*
*Stage 4: Launch // Semi-Supportive*

## Stage 1: Pre-Launch

This is your time of recruiting team members, raising financial support, developing strategy with your team, and planning. This stage will usually last one to two years and will likely be your leanest budgeted stage. You will probably need to have a job during this time, and most of the money will go to development.

You have to make an important decision during this stage. That decision is if you will work in your current job, work in the community part-time, or if you will head off to plan, recruit, and fundraise full-time.

There are pros and cons to each of these options.

The advantages of working in the community you will plant is the relationships and connections you will make. I told you the story of Scott Bruegman in Denver. He got a part-time job working at a hospital doing some chaplain duties. He also started a nonprofit that connected with kids and their parents. If you were to ask him if he felt these two opportunities were beneficial to the success of the church-plant, he would answer, "yes!"

A disadvantage to working in the community is that you will need less money, but you will need it for a LONGER time.

Choosing to fundraise full-time is a much more risky approach but can accelerate the speed in which you will be able to develop a team, strategy, and finances for the vision. A challenge to full-time fundraising is you will need money for not as long, but you will need MORE money.

You just have to make a decision on what you will do during this stage. You might have a personal value and vision to not be employed at all by the church, or for any of the staff to be, even when the church is self-supportive. There are definitely advantages and teachings out there that say this is a way to go. The bi-vocational pastor has made a resurgence, and not just for smaller churches.

I am going to assume you will make the decision to eventually see yourself as the pastor and some of your team members on paid staff as the church grows and becomes more self-sustaining financially. I am assuming this because this is the majority of the church planters I have encountered.

Once you have settled the issue of financial support, your next step is to come up with a personal budget for what it will take to be full-time with your church-plant. You have to understand where you are and where you are headed. Begin with the bare essentials and work from there based on what financial resources you have available to you.

**Personal Budget:**

*Housing Cost*

*Utilities*

*Food*

*Household products*

*Car*

*Gas*

*Cell Phones*

*Health Insurance*

*Kids Needs*

*Bills (Work to take care of any debt before you plant.)*

Notice what is not on here: play money. Don't over budget on your personal expenses up front, get the process going and go on the bare side of life until you get to future stages.

Once you find out what you need per month, as well as what costs you will need to start the development of your church planting (we will call that your work budget), then you should have an idea of a rough budget.

**Work Budget:**

*Travel to potential donors*
*Travel to potential team members*
*Newsletters to donors*
*Website creation and maintenance*
*Recruiting money*
*Taxes and fees for church registration*

In your personal budget, I asked you to think in terms of bare essentials. In your work budget, I could encourage you to double (maybe even triple) whatever you budget for the above categories. It's been my experience that while you can always live on less, it will cost a lot more than you think to get things started with your new church-plant.

### Stage 2: Pre-Launch // Ministry

This is the stage in which you should have raised your pre-launch budget and have recruited team members to join your team. Your team will now start to reach out to the community to start building relationships, build the identity of the new church community, and begin discipleship with those they are leading to Jesus. There is no formal PUBLIC gathering or services at this point. Everything is very grass roots and organic.

Your personal budget will not change, but you will add to your work budget in this stage.

**Work Budget:**

*Bibles and discipleship materials*
*Food for smaller gatherings*
*Branding of church name and identity*

Stage 2 will vary on its duration. The longer you allow Stage 2 to go, the better chance of health your new Jesus community will have in the long run. This time period is almost like the nine-month pregnancy period for women. It allows time for the mom to prepare and for the new baby to grow healthy and strong.

If Stage 1 is about getting pregnant, then Stage 2 is about being pregnant. Hopefully, you will keep your hand on the pulse of the new relationships and discipleship that is taking place in the new church. This will give you a pulse on when you are to send everyone out to start multiplying themselves within the community.

I have seen this stage last up to three years for some churches. Again, it will vary.

One such church-plant that I was semi-connected with took almost two years of meeting in a barn once a week to connect with the team they had recruited, the core group that had formed, and the people they had built relationships with. For almost two years they taught about what church was and what it wasn't, about what discipleship was and what it wasn't. Then they marketed themselves to the area when they were getting ready to let the public know who they were. When they officially launched, they had such a strong healthy core that their birth weight was sizable and they are doing great at reaching people for Jesus.

Another church-plant I watched develop did a house church for almost two and a half years before they took their trained team members from that house church and sent them out to start other house churches. They now have over eight house churches with five years of ministry, and almost every person in these house churches is a brand new follower of Jesus.

Be careful that you don't get comfortable in this stage. You can start to wear down your donors and team members. Talk of what is going to be will only take you so far; you have to put flesh on the vision for people to follow you after so long of vision casting. You can stay in Stage 2 for a long time and then find yourself giving birth to a stillborn. No one will want to move on from where you are at because all they know is addition ministry and theorizing about multiplication ministry. You want to make disciples who are making disciples. If you make disciples who just love being a disciple with no intention of ever passing it on to anyone else, you will eventually stall out.

## Stage 3: Launch // Infancy

Stage 3 is a fun stage. It is a lot of work but very exciting. This is where your team and all the new followers of Jesus who have been gathering in Stage 2 are now turned lose in the community to start multiplying. This is usually the stage where you launch your public services or gatherings or cell ministry or house churches. Whatever you have decided and feel God has placed inside of you as the multiplication piece of making disciples, this will be your launch stage.

At every stage, you will need to make adjustments to your budget. A budget is just a guide. You have to make certain assumptions about cost, number of people, and the speed in which you will move. In the beginning, you will be making many tweaks along the way based on needs, people, and financial support.

Hopefully during Stage 2 you have started to teach your team members, core team, and new followers of Jesus about giving. If you have been putting this money aside then you will be able to use this money for your work budget during Stage 3, which will last usually about one year. Maybe two years in a very hard demographic, such as inner city work or rural America.

### Stage 4: Launch // Semi-Supportive

This stage begins when you hit a point where the new Jesus community is giving enough funds to cover the work budget that it needs to operate and starting to handle the personal budget of the pastor and team members' stipends. It should be simple to figure out: the amount you need from donors at this point is the difference between your needs and what is currently being given.

Your goal should always be for the new Jesus community to handle its own financial load and responsibility.

# How to Raise Funds

So you have your budget in place and you understand what amount of money you need to raise. You have an idea of the development lifecycle of your new church-plant and when you will need a particular level of financial assistance. Now it's time to actually get the money from donors.

Let me just tell you that there is formal training available that will teach you the depth and details to this process I am about to give to you if you're interested. I personally am the lead facilitator for a class given twice a year for the Assemblies of God U.S. Missions. I've helped them rewrite the materials to keep them current. This subject could be a book in and of itself, but I want to give you something to work with right now.

With all of that in mind, what I am about to outline for you is what I learned from Henri Moreau, personal experience, and what I have seen work for more than one hundred church-plants, hundreds of missionaries, and scores of nonprofits. This isn't theory but advice that has a proven track record.

*1. Budget*

We covered that; we know what we need, and when we need it. Don't ask for more than you will need at a given time. Donors will give more down the road when they see you use what you asked for in an efficient manner. Don't ever allow yourself to be perceived as asking for money without a specific need and a plan to use those funds. You're not the only one asking for money from the people who can financially support you.

## 2. Brainstorm

Who are the people you know who believe in you? Friends, former church attendees, pastors, churches, personal doctors and dentists, former teachers, neighbors, relatives, Facebook friends, etc. Include everyone you can think of who you have a connection with. Don't worry if they don't believe like you do; it is about them believing in you. I have seen people of other faiths give to evangelical church planters because they see the heart in which the planter is going to take into a community.

Compile this list of individuals. Track down their addresses, e-mail addresses, phone numbers, Facebook accounts, etc.

Create a database of these individuals and churches. I use a great free program called TNTmpd. You can download this from the Internet at www.tntware.com. Others I know create their own excel spreadsheet or buy programs for databases. It doesn't matter; just make a database you can oversee and work with. Organization is KEY.

## 3. Pre-Appointment Letters

We have all received blind letters asking for money from people we don't know or barely know. I sent out four hundred of them at the beginning stages of our fundraising, but these don't work as effectively as ones sent to people with whom you have an existing relationship.

Take your organized data and begin to send out personalized letters telling your potential donors about your church-plant. In fact let's stop calling them donors . . . let's call them partners. They are going to partner with you to fulfill the vision God has placed inside of you.

You are going to send a letter out to your potential partners telling them about the vision God has given you, and you are going to tell them that you are in need of partners to help financially support this vision. You are also going to tell them that you will be calling them to set-up a face-to-face meeting where you will share this vision with them. Your goal in writing this letter is to prepare them for an appointment. Keep the letter personal, no longer than one page, and to the point.

One key suggestion I would tell you is this: Send out twenty to thirty letters at a time. The next week follow-up on them and then send out another twenty to thirty letters to more potential partners.

*Example Letter*

*[Please write your own ending. Don't steal this one. The last thing you need is everyone getting the same paragraph across the country that is impersonal and not from you. Everyone uses Google.]*

Dear _____,

*[Paragraph one includes a personal connection and introduction.]*
I think I saw you last at your wedding. I can't believe three years have gone by so fast. I knew things were going to change when you

got married—sure miss our boys' nights out, but I know you are now in better company than with me.

*[Paragraph two shares the vision of what you will be setting out to do.]*
Anyways, I am writing you to share what Cindy and I are up to these days. Actually, it isn't what we are up to but more of what we are about our upcoming adventure. In the next year we are moving to Sacramento to begin work on starting a new church in the downtown area. We have felt compelled by God to move our family there to be His hands and feet to the people of downtown Sacramento. We never saw ourselves as Californians or living downtown in any city, but on a recent visit to Sacramento we felt overwhelmed with giving up everything to spread the love of God to those who are in need of it there.

*[Paragraph three explains the reason for your letter.]*
We cannot accomplish this vision that God has given us alone. We are actively praying and asking God to guide us to ministry partners who will financially support and pray for this new church community as it gets on its feet. We want to ask you to consider being one of our partners in ministry. We will be calling you next week to set up a time when we can meet with you in person to share this vision and talk to you about what it means to partner with us. We look forward to connecting with you next week on the phone and finally getting a chance to sit down with you in person.

In Christ,
Billy the Church Planter

*4. Phone Call*

A week after you send out the letters, call your contacts! If you tell them you will call in a week, call them that NEXT WEEK! If you can't get in touch with them on the phone, leave a voicemail. Don't expect anyone to ever call you back. This is on YOU, not them. Be persistent and keep trying to connect with them. Use e-mail or Facebook to set up a time to call them on the phone, but get them on the phone. The more personal you can make your conversation the better.

Once you get them on the phone, your goal is get an APPOINT-MENT to meet with them in person. This goes for individuals, pastors, and nonprofits. Whoever you are talking to, get an appointment. Once you have one scheduled, hang up. (Not really. Just don't try to do too much in one step.)

*Sample Phone Call*

"Hey, is Joey there?"

"Speaking."

"Joey, this is Billy. It is so great to hear your voice. I think about you every time I see the Cubs on TV."

"You know that is always a sore spot in my heart; you had to poke at it."

"Ha, ha. You know I like to keep you humble."

"That's what I love about you."

"Did you get my letter I sent you last week?"

"Sure did, Billy. Sounds like you got some exciting things going on, thanks for sharing with me."

"I appreciate that. Well, as I said in the letter Joey, Cindy and I would really like to meet with you in person and share this new adventure with you as well as talk to you about how you can be part of this next stage in our lives."

"It would be great to catch up."

"Of course it would be. How is next Monday night for you and your wife? Can we take you to dinner?"

"Next Monday night doesn't work, but what about Tuesday night?"

"That works! Let's do it."

"Alright."

"How about we meet at the new steakhouse on the corner of Main and 4th at 6:30 p.m.?"

"Okay, it's a double date! See you then."

"Bye!"

Once you get your contact on the phone, build rapport. You are not selling anything; you are seeking out people who will buy in to you and believe in you. People will invest their money and prayers in those they believe in, but they will never give when feeling sold to. This goes for churches and pastors too.

After you build rapport, then reference the letter you sent. If for some reason they didn't get the letter or read it, no worries. Just paraphrase the letter and move onto the next part of the phone call. You will want to reference why you want to meet with them. Even if they have read the letter, make sure you tell them you are looking for ministry partners to support this endeavor. You don't ever want anyone to feel like you deceived them.

Next you will want to ask about a specific time to meet with them. Don't generalize about a time, "Hey how is meeting up next week?" If it is a couple or someone who works full-time, then meeting in the afternoons and evenings will be the best. If you are talking to a church leader or pastor, then coffee or a meeting at their office during the day will be the best. If you get hesitation about the amount of time it will take, assure them it will be a max of thirty minutes.

After you have set a time and date for the meeting, confirm and close out the phone call. Keep the phone call short and to the point. Sometimes you will be having this phone call with a church leader's administrative assistant, so be prepared to talk to anyone and everyone on the phone. (Just because she is an administrative assistant doesn't mean she isn't married to the wealthiest man in town. You never know the giving capacity of the people you're talking to. Treat everyone as though God might use them to fund your new church-plant.)

*5. The Meeting*

Make sure you show up on time to the place you agreed to meet. Don't be late. Have all of your materials with you. You will want to bring pictures of the place you are going to start the new church community if it is unfamiliar to your potential donor and any packet information that you might have made. You will also want to create some sort of pledge form that allows your partners to sign an agreement on a monthly amount of money they are willing to give or agree to a date at which they'll give a one-time amount. Make them feel like a ministry partner, not a charitable giver.

Prepare a thirty-minute presentation to share how God called you to this vision, what you will be doing, and how it will impact people. Also use this opportunity to convey a story of someone coming to know Jesus and how his or her life is now different because of it. Get this story of someone finding Jesus from other church planters or from someone you personally helped discover Jesus. We are results-based in our giving and partnership. If your potential partner can see the fruit of what could be with a real story, they are more likely to partner with you.

*6. Ask*

Whether you are sitting in front of a lifelong friend or a pastor of a church, at the end of your presentation time you will have to finally get to the point of asking them to partner with you. You can't just ask someone to be a partner; you will want to ask them to do something in that partnership. Be specific.

"Pastor Alex, I really would love for you and your church to partner with us in this endeavor with prayer and helping us on a monthly basis financially. We have put together a budget for this first stage of our church-plant and we would ask that you prayerfully consider giving five hundred dollars a month."

You will probably ask for higher amount from churches than you will from individuals. You will know roughly what an individual can do and how well off a church can help you. For monthly pledges: $50–$100 is a good number to ask an individual; $100–$1,000 is a good number to ask a church. For one-time gifts: $200–$1,000 is a good number to ask an individual; $1,000–$10,000 is a good number to ask a church.

If you ask higher than they can give, they will always tell you a lower number. In other words, if you ask an individual for $100 a month, they might say, I can't do $100, but I can do $50 a month. BUT if you ask for $50 a month and they could have done $100 a month, they will almost NEVER go up. They will give you the lower number that you asked for. Err on the side of asking for what you want.

I personally like the monthly pledges because it is easier for a church or individual to commit to upfront and sustain over the four stages we outlined above. However, it does mean that you must keep up with sending monthly reminders or contribution statements.

Once you make the ask, shut up. You will want to keep talking. Resist that urge. Let them respond. The next words that come out of anyone's mouth should be from your potential partner.

We get nervous with silence, and we can talk ourselves out of a partner. I am willing to bet you that almost 95 percent of the churches and people you meet with want to partner with you, but in that time of silence after you have asked, they are processing their current financial commitments and listening to any promptings they are getting from God.

If they say no, don't worry. God will provide you other partners.

If they say yes, then pull out your pledge form and get them to fill it out right then and there. Your next question will be when they can make their first donation. Make note of this and send your reminder for them to give at that time.

I saw one church planter make a payment book like a car loan company does; it worked out awesome for them in getting their financial commitments on time. You will also want to let them know that you will be sending them newsletters to keep them up on what is going on with the ministry.

## 7. Follow Up

Whether they say yes or no to partnering with you, make sure you always send a thank you card within the next two to three days of your meeting. This isn't about selling anything; these are relationships with people.

Make sure you send out reminders about the commitments your partners have made. Don't get embarrassed about doing this either. Some people simply forget with the busy life they lead, and just like if you made a commitment, a friendly reminder would not be insulting to you.

## 8. Send Regular Communication

The number one reason people stop supporting nonprofits, missionaries, and church-plants is that they don't hear from them anymore. My advice is for you to start sending out newsletters once a month to your partners. You can always send out quarterly newsletters to those who are interested in what you're doing but not financially supporting you. Remember, a no today doesn't mean a no forever. Your newsletter can be electronic or printed; it's your preference.

Beyond newsletters, make sure you are personally connecting with your partners. Send them personal e-mails, call them every once in a while, ask them what you can be in prayer for in their life and church, and send them gifts. If you treat them special, they will feel special and will not leave your side. If they know they matter, they will stay with you during this long hard process.

This is the difference between those who have financial partners and those who don't.

## 9. Referrals

I lived on referrals. After meeting with individuals and pastors face-to-face, I realized I needed something more than just my own contact list. I had already run though some of the list by sending out that first wave of four hundred letters.

So, I began to ask each of my partners, "Can you recommend three [people/churches/pastors] I can contact and tell them you gave me their names because you thought they'd be interested in what we are doing and potentially want to partner with us as well?"

I ended up meeting so many pastors and churches across the United States because of this. Businessmen and businesswomen who had a heart for what I was doing but would never have been introduced to me if I hadn't asked this question. You might not even know your biggest partners yet.

## 10. The Last 5%

As I was discussing this chapter with my mentor, who is one of the elders of our church, he shared his belief that most generous people and church-plants attract generous partners.

I agree.

You reap what you sow.

If you are ungiving and stingy with partnering in church-plants and missions, don't expect others to give to your new church community. A generous heart is infectious.

Give personally and give from the very beginning with your new church community. You will sow generosity that will be a great harvest.

I was sitting down with one of our partnering church pastors having lunch with him about three months into our journey. He told me how the church handled their giving to projects like ours and he began to tell me how a few years back his church made a decision to tithe as a church. They would set aside 10 percent of all contributions to be given away to other churches and missions. This church had no debt or financial struggles.

I thought to myself, *Well they have no debt or struggles, so they are able to do that.* Then it dawned on me that it was the reverse. They never went without because they were always willing to give and bless others.

From the day we started taking in money at Elevation Church, we have set aside 10 percent of everything to send right back out our doors through generous giving. Half of it goes to help church-plants like we once were, and the other half goes to missions and social justice projects across the globe.

I have sat on church planting committees and boards where we were given the responsibility of overseeing church planting funds for new church-plants. During the different stages of these church-plants they would ask us for money from the fund. I was always willing to say yes to their requests if we could see that the church as well as its leaders were generous themselves. It was as if our giving from this fund wasn't going to just help out this one church or ministry, but it would flow through them to others as well, and would have a bigger impact around the world.

It goes beyond the church though.

If you can't give in your personal life, if you struggle with having a generous heart personally, then you will struggle with giving as a church and receiving from others.

Generosity follows generosity.

If you hold on to your own money with a tight fist, you will never know how to open your hand to let God pour more into it. Maybe there are different books and teachings you should be going through right now other than how to raise money.

May God give us a generous heart. May the nerve between our pocket book and our heart be severed so we might be released to give to others besides ourselves. Amen!

# Chapter Seven in Review

*Key Ideas*

1. All new church-plants must be funded.
2. The establishment of the new church will require a detailed budget and a plan to obtain support.
3. The church-planter must exhibit the same personal financial responsibility as he expects his church to exhibit.
4. One key to effective fundraising is building rapport.
5. Generosity is contagious.

*Discussion Questions*

1. How do you plan to fund your new church?
2. Describe your budgeting process. What categories or expenses do you see as predictable and which are unpredictable? How will you plan for each?
3. How would you rate your handling of your personal finances? If your church mirrors your personal finances, how stable will it be?
4. How can you build rapport with potential donors?
5. What are three ways you can demonstrate generosity without appearing to be boastful?

*Next Steps*

1. Begin developing a comprehensive ministry plan for the establishment of the church.
2. Create action steps related to your budget. Make the action steps realistic and obtainable.

3. Evaluate your personal finances and look for ways to demonstrate faithfulness and generosity in your own life.
4. Develop a strategy for building relationships with influential people in your new community.
5. Periodically celebrate generosity through your leadership team.

# CHAPTER 8

# THIS WILL SAVE YOU SOME MAJOR HEADACHES

*"You need to decide now where you stand with
your idea of church polity."*

One of the biggest things I never processed at the beginning stages of our new church community was how we would decide if someone is a leader in our church, what the process is for becoming a leader, and what the qualifications of such leaders should be.

At the early stages, being a leader in our church was based on being a follower of Jesus and their buy-in to the vision for our church community. It was all based on personal relationships, and we all knew each other inside and out in the early stages. As the church community grew, I wasn't connected with every person as intimately as I was in the beginning. How was I to process who was leadership material and what standards I would use to develop a reproducible leadership model? It was completely based on my relationships.

Remember the story I told you about the house church leader who was teaching some pretty opinionated theology to his group in chapter 5? Here was a classic sign of my problem. This guy attended our church, came to me saying that he wanted to be a leader, had great qualifications under his belt, and was a likable guy. We found out later on that this guy had very different theological beliefs than we did and was spouting these beliefs as the standards of our church community. This could have been lethal for us as a community.

As our house churches started to grow and as our Sunday services began to grow, we started having more and more people come to us saying that they wanted to lead a house church too. We had to sit down and process how someone in our community could become a leader we can endorse and trust to lead others the way we were leading them.

We started talking to other churches that were farther along the road than us—specifically, churches that had to start from scratch like we did. It took a lot of experimentation to refine our process, but this is what we came up with.

### How to Decide Who Is a Leader

Leaders were defined as those who were teaching others how to follow Jesus in some sort of group gathering or one-on-one meeting with the trust of the whole community.

*1. Most have attended our church for at least six months and have been a follower of Jesus for at least a year.*

We found that if someone was a new follower of Jesus they had such a fire burning in them at the very beginning of their conversion that they wanted to emulate the leaders who were guiding them. The problem we found was that they would burn out really fast if we gave them too much too fast OR they would not have developed the spiritual maturity to walk the narrow road that was following Jesus.

We also found that we needed someone to really know who we were, and we needed to know who they were. You could see this in people when they just spent time in our community—not leading, not doing anything . . . but just being! It was such a interesting process for us to watch people come into the church community, express a desire to lead, and ask them to just hang for at least six months. We could see the true heart of an individual during that period of observation.

Those who struggled with just serving and being never became a leader and eventually left. Those who didn't blink really cared about the relationships they were building and the vision of the church.

*2. Most attend our Joining the Journey class and sign a covenant officially joining our community.*

Our *Joining the Journey* class lasts for one hour once a week for ten weeks. We discovered that if we shortened the class or tried to cram everything into a weekend, the process produced less devoted individuals in the end.

We are not sociologists, but we felt that when we made the class a longer commitment and people jumped through that commitment, then they developed a greater sense of community, connection, and purpose. It was harder for them to abandon the people they had spent such a long time interacting with during those ten weeks. (It's probably the same reason why Dave Ramsey makes his class thirteen weeks long.)

The class itself covers our five DNA traits, our values, and our beliefs as a Jesus community. We specifically cover the theological issues we consider "close-handed" issues or, as some would say, "nonnegotiables."

Someone who attends the *Joining the Journey* class will have a complete understanding of who we are as a church, and we usually uncover their own personal beliefs or past church teachings during that time period.

For us, we believe in all the spiritual gifts. When we get to this part of the teaching in the *Joining the Journey* class, we are made aware almost instantly where someone falls on this issue.

Now as a general rule, I am usually almost always talking about people who are followers of Jesus before they start attending our church community. New followers of Jesus never really push back on the beliefs but seek to understand them more. These new followers of Jesus usually always see the class as a foundational beliefs class in understanding the major theological points of the Bible and the culture of our community.

I remember one class in particular that I was teaching where a couple expressed a desire to be leaders in our church. They were checking the *Joining the Journey* class off of their list, jumping through the hoops so to speak. One of our classes focuses on generosity and, specifically, tithing. This couple began to spout off at how they don't believe tithing is a New Testament principle. Though they eventually finished the classes and signed the covenant, we were aware of their views on this issue. It probably wouldn't be wise to put them in a position that deals with the finances if we know this about them, but we were able to discover this because of our extensive *Joining the Journey* class.

The covenant has been really handy too.

It is a very basic covenant, but we found that when we ask people to sign it, it brings out the importance of being a leader in the Jesus community. We don't take it lightly. In our American culture, we sign things that have importance and value. Asking someone to put their name to a covenant speaks to that cultural understanding of importance and value.

We ask them to commit to the following in our covenant:

1. Following Jesus Christ. *He is my Savior, my Master, my Lord, my Everything. I am on a journey with Jesus and I will strive to love Him with my mind, my inner being, my heart, and all of my strength.*

2. Loving Others in the Community. *Together I am stronger than I am alone. We need each other. I will be there for other people at Elevation Church.*

3. Loving My World. *People who live around me need my smiles, jokes, prayers, hands, and friendship. Jesus died for people; they are the most important things on this Earth.*

4. Giving My Time. *Our community will not exist without my help. I am committed to giving valuable time to seeing our common goals achieved.*

5. Giving My Resources. *I will put my talents, possessions, and money where my mouth is to help support this community.*

6. I Am the Church. *God's church is not an organization or denomination; it is people like me who follow Him. I am committed to being who He created me to be and being His hands on Earth.*

This covenant has been a barrier to some people. They attend the class but never sign the covenant. They don't want to carry the expectations we have of those who identify as members of our Jesus community. That is fine with us. We don't want people to lead who don't want us to have expectations of them.

*3. They must apprentice with someone for a minimum of three months before leading something on their own.*

You might think that we have a ton of "hoops." The last part doesn't necessarily have to happen after the *Joining the Journey* class but just needs to happen. We want to have a current leader pour into them. Maybe the leader who is pouring into them is not a better leader than the one who is apprenticing; it is more about them serving in a servant-leadership role. We want the leaders in our church community to have within them the heart of supporting each other, not having a mindset that "everything is about me."

We say it all the time at our church that we are not IT, but we are *part* of IT. We want the same to be true for individual leaders. IT isn't about them, but they are part of making IT happen. The most basic level of leadership happens when someone does these three things and our current leadership recognizes the desire that he has to be a leader coupled with the presence of God evident in his life.

I wish someone had shared these things with me before we ventured out into church planting. I envisioned leaders but didn't think through a process to not only train but sift through the people who would want to be leaders.

You need a process and training.
You don't need it after year one.
You don't need to come up with it on the fly.
You need it now!

Even if you haven't started, you need to formulate something today. You can tweak it down the road, but it's essential to have a process you can follow as you walk through the beginning stages of church planting.

BUT leadership goes beyond just creating a process on leadership development and discovery.

What about all those core team members you recruited? When there are five of you, you will play leadership like a basketball team. The leader serves as the point guard and everyone else plays a position that they are good at. Most of the time you run around doing the similar things.

As you start adding more leaders to the equation, you can't play ball the same way.

You are going to need to develop a flow chart of how your team is going to play as more people join your leadership and you grow. Develop this as what you WANT it to be today. You can always change it up as your community and leadership base grows.

After we developed a leadership process, we developed a flow chart of expectations and responsibilities of our team with these new leaders.

These flow charts keep changing as we keep growing, but they really help us when we sit down with new leaders and show them how the leadership of the church plays itself out.

**Decide Now How You Will Govern Your Church**

Maybe I am an idiot or just dumb, but I honestly never thought about church polity (governance) until I was about two years into our church-plant. Our church-planting network assigned leaders to oversee our church from a spiritual and legal perspective. I just assumed (which was wrong of me) that there would be a great process that would help us transition into governing ourselves.

Your church-planting network or denomination will probably have something similar for you at the beginning of the church's life, but you need to have a rough sketch in your mind of what the church governance will eventually look like. There are lots of different ways in which your church can be set-up in its governance, and you will need to plan at the front end for it to take place. We didn't and by the time we did, it took us almost another two years to formulate the new governance idea throughout the whole culture of the church.

You need to decide now where you stand with your idea of church polity, especially from a theological perspective. The three most common set-ups for church governance are congregational led, elder/board led, or pastor led. All of these have their pros and cons.

## 1. Congregational-Led Churches

The congregational-led church is probably the most popular and the one that you are most familiar with, especially if you come from an evangelical background.

Congregational-led churches have an "American democracy" feel to them. The priesthood-of-all-believers concept is translated into all having a say in the direction and governance of the church. Congregational churches give membership to congregants, and with this membership comes voting power to approve bylaws, church legal business, legal board approvals, staff hiring decisions, and sometimes even church policy and theological decisions.

The pros of this style are the involvement of many, the buy-in of the community, and the accountability that naturally comes when everyone needs to know the inner workings to make a decision in their votes. Ownership seems to come easy to those in a congregational style.

The cons can be fractured relationships within the congregation over preference or disputes within the governing bodies. When everyone feels like they get a say, if they are not heard or approved, they can feel hurt, especially when you are dealing with personal issues of faith.

### 2. Elder/Board-Led Churches

Elder/Board-led churches are based on either two different styles. Board-led churches have more of a CEO/business feel to them. The governance style that works for Fortune 500 companies is woven into the church governance. Elder-led churches have a similar make-up but usually the difference is in how the board or elders are selected, their stated qualifications, and how they are given responsibilities.

Generally, you will see board-led churches give their board members legal and decision-making responsibilities, whereas elder-led churches will give their elders not only those same responsibilities but add on the authority of watching over the spiritual health of the church and actively teaching, preaching, and ministering in the church. Think of it as board-led churches being a decision-making body and elder-led churches being a ministering body.

Though there is no specific church governance style outlined in the pages of Scripture, there is more biblical evidence for the elder-led style than any other. Paul, in his various writings to Timothy and Titus, helps them to set up church leadership and authority. He refers to elders, or overseers, who will govern the church on a local level.

### 3. Pastor-Led Churches

Pastor-led churches are probably the least common. The pastor holds all the legal, decision-making, and spiritual authority in the church. Think of it as business with one owner. I am the least familiar with this style, as I have found through the pages of Scripture that we were never to do anything alone. Though I don't think there is any completely wrong way to govern a church, I think that you can have a governance that sets you up for failure. This would be one of those areas that I think has the potential to rely too much on one, fallen man. Accountability in leadership and governance is important.

I suggest you decide ahead of time which style fits your theological perspective and your team's concept of what leadership will look like in your Jesus community. Find other churches that have similar views of church governance that you have and ask them for their bylaws. Ask the pastor what they would do different if they could do it all over again.

We started to collect bylaws from churches that were elder-led when we felt like the pages of Scripture pointed us to that governance style. After collecting four bylaws and talking to the pastors of those churches, we were able to put together bylaws that really reflected us and who we felt God had called us to be.

I will give you two pieces of advice for your bylaws that I learned in getting ours put together. First, keep it simple. Longer isn't better. Put together a simple legal document that outlines the governance of the church community. Second, don't legislate policy. Don't stick every little legal way you do things in your bylaws. Create a policy manual that you can change as a leadership team easily. You will find that as times and people change, some of the decisions you have made in the way you do things will need to be tweaked. Don't bind yourself in your bylaws when you don't have to. Your bylaws should bind what is a deal breaker, not what is just a decision on the way you do things in your current administration of the church. Remember, whatever system you set up for your governance and administration, it is there to serve YOU, not for you to serve IT. The system serves us—we don't serve the system.

I'm telling you that if you think through this NOW, you will save yourself a lot of headaches down the road. If God ever sends me out to plant a church again, this will be the chapter I revisit first.

# CHAPTER EIGHT IN REVIEW

*Key Ideas*

1. Leaders must be committed followers of Jesus Christ.
2. Church planters must establish and enforce leadership requirements and restrictions.
3. Churches should develop a leadership covenant and require all leaders to sign it.
4. The development of your church will require more leaders; therefore, an apprentice program is vital.
5. All churches must choose a church governance model.

*Discussion Questions*

1. How do you know if a potential leader is really an authentic follower of Jesus Christ or not?
2. What personal beliefs and/or habits might disqualify someone from a leadership role in your church? Why are these deal-breakers?
3. What are the elements of an effective leadership covenant?
4. Why is an apprentice leader program vital to your church's future health?
5. Which church governance model is most palatable to you? Why?

*Next Steps*

1. List interview questions you will use in conversation with all potential leaders.
2. Identify the elements of a leadership covenant and begin developing it.

3. Develop a redemptive plan for dealing with people who are disqualified from leadership.
4. Look for an apprentice to partner with you so you can model the process for other leaders.
5. Evaluate the church governance model and select the one that give you the greatest freedom to lead the church as God leads you.

# CHAPTER 9

# THE 11TH COMMANDMENT IS THIS: TEACH DOCTRINE EARLY AND OFTEN

*"Transformation will take place when the age-old principles of spiritual habits are taught and incorporated into someone's life."*

The house was packed that night. New people seemed to show up every week. There was nothing special about this Bible study and small group. There was no super creative illustrations used every week. There was no video series being played. There was no catered meal.

It was an honest discussion and study of the Bible and how it applied to life. Discipleship was taking place. One person would find Jesus, mature in their understanding and life with God, and then share the experience with someone else.

It just seemed to be happening faster than normal.

The crowd settled down from the normal chit-chat that would naturally take place as everyone arrived. Individual conversations that had sprung up around the room were closed with a period as focus was drawn to the Bible study leader for the evening. The leader offered up a prayer for the evening and quickly dived into the discussion for the night.

He began by giving an overview of where they had been studying in the past weeks, the Gospel of John, and what they had summarized and learned. He was careful with his words. Knowing that most of the people in the room had not been there each week to hear all of the discussions and teachings. Just as most discipleship happens in a healthy church, one-on-one learning was taking place. An in-depth Bible study was being added to their diet, on top of the Sunday worship services with everyone in the Jesus community.

The leader quickly referenced Paul as he was heading into the meat of the Bible study, "Now remember what Paul said when he talked about us doing this on our own: if we could do this on our own, then we didn't need Jesus to die for us."

A hand quickly shot up from the crowd.

"You don't have to raise your hand to ask a question here."

"Sorry. I just don't know what to do. Okay, so here is my question. If this guy Paul has such a deep understanding of the Bible and what Jesus did and didn't do, I would really like to meet him. You guys refer to him all the time. What service does Paul go to at our church?"

What service does Paul go to?

I will always remember this phrase. It reminds me of what you and I are supposed to be doing—teaching others about the way of Jesus.

From nothing to something.
From infancy to maturity.

If discipleship is our goal, and it is, then infant-sounding questions should ring as celebration of the message of Jesus being wanted and planted into the heart of new followers. But (and there is always a big but) the questions shouldn't stay infant questions. If we are making disciples, they should be moving to maturity.

### Grow Disciples

Just as my daughter used to ask me, "What are the white things in the sky?" I have taught her the answer and her question has now changed to, "Is that a stratus cloud, Daddy?"

The only way you are going to move a person from infancy to maturity is to TEACH THEM.

Church planter, I know what you will focus on. I know you will do everything possible to attract the crowds. If you have success attracting crowds to your service in one method, you will go back to that method as your bread and butter.

I mean, it kind of makes sense right?
The church is a living organism. Healthy organisms grow. So a growing church is a healthy church, right?

NOT!

Discipleship is about transformed lives.

Discipleship is about teaching others the way of Jesus.

We all want to see it multiply out: disciples making disciples.

Crowds are not disciples. Sorry.

The best thing you can do as a church planter is to learn from other churches that have gone before you and make sure that you are committed to depth, not width. If you are not careful, one day you will wake up in a kiddie pool that is two miles wide and two inches deep.

## Teach Biblical Doctrine

Start off your church-plant on the right trajectory by making sure you teach biblical doctrine early and often.

I know some of you just read the word *doctrine* and thought to yourself, *What? No way! It will scare all the new converts off.*

That is what I thought too.

We kicked off our services with sermons on how Christianity was relevant, on exploring the Advent, on the fruits of the Spirit, etc. After the first year, we started to look around and see that all of the people who were coming to know Jesus would take what we said in the Sunday services as what was most important for us to know. They would end up in their house churches saying things like, "We haven't ever talked about that on a Sunday. I'm sure if it was that important we wouldn't have all learned that together."

It dawned on our leadership that we set a foundation in the larger gatherings of what the standard was in our faith as followers of Jesus. We realized that what we did in our large gatherings had to simulate almost what was happening and being taught in the house churches and one-on-one discipleship.

What were we willing to die for?
That is what we should be teaching.

What is the gospel message?
That is what needs to be taught.

Grace.
Redemption.
God in the flesh.
Salvation through Christ's sacrifice.
God working through us.
Obedience to His words.
Following after Jesus.

These things needed to be . . .

. . . taught,
. . . discussed,
. . . and pondered.

Early. And. Often.

The bottom line is this: You will have so many people show up to your services who will never go to a small group. They will never go to a one-on-one discipleship meeting. They will faithfully attend and even consider themselves part of your church community. The large gatherings and services you hold might be their only chance to have seeds of the gospel planted into their souls.

Likewise, you will have very devoted small group members and maturing followers of Jesus who will attend large gatherings and services faithfully too. What you teach will give them a compass to living out their faith with Jesus.

What you teach in your main gatherings will be a doorway. You will set the stage for what is important by what you teach publicly in your large gatherings. If you teach good, sound doctrine, you will direct people. That's what proper doctrine does—it leads us.

Our leadership team made the decision that we were going to teach the Bible. We would take whole books, if not large chunks of the Bible, and teach what it was saying. It wasn't that we became expositors of Scripture; it was that we became "exposi-topical" teachers of the gospel of Jesus.

Could we teach others what the Bible said, how it all fit together, and how they could find it on their own? Could we teach others the deep truths of the gospel in our large gatherings, hoping that it would lead to spiritual growth in their smaller groups and one-on-one discipleship? Could we teach others what was expected of a life of a follower of Jesus? Could we teach them to maybe feed themselves?

I was discussing this with a mentor of mine, who told me the story of Willow Creek Community Church in the Chicago area. Willow Creek did this big study with a bunch of other churches on the spiritual growth of individuals, and at the end they had to face some hard truths. They named the study REVEAL, for the obvious—it revealed to them something they were not expecting.

This is what was revealed in Willow Creek's study, in a nutshell:

Growth of a church, specifically attendance, did not mean that there was spiritual growth in those who attended. ALSO, someone's activity in a church, volunteering and serving, did not affect spiritual growth.

So a study conducted by one of the largest and marquee churches in America taught us all that attracting people to a large gathering did not translate into transformed spiritual growth.

The pastor of Willow Creek, Bill Hybels, summarized the study like this: Some of the stuff that they had put millions of dollars into thinking would really help their people grow and develop spiritually, wasn't helping them do so. Other things that they didn't put that much money into and didn't commit much staff leadership to is what their people were crying out for. (I didn't put this in quotes because it's not a word-for-word account. I think you get my point.)

My biggest take away from listening to Bill Hybels talk at a leadership summit on this study came when he admitted they had made some mistakes and wished they had done things differently. But I don't think this commentary can only be said about Willow Creek. There are a lot of churches who haven't been putting their focus on, and investing in, the things that last for eternity. Spiritual maturity should always be the goal.

What Hybels described was making disciples.

Church planter, you cannot expect people to want to feed themselves unless they understand that Jesus is God, that the Bible is the Word of God, that grace alone saves them because of the redemptive work on the cross. Don't give them feel-good messages and teachings. TEACH them TRUTH. I'm not saying a seeker-sensitive message series is a no-no; you just need to make it a habit of teaching doctrine and teaching often. Teach spiritual habits often.

Anyone can attract a crowd. That guy down in Florida who claims to be Jesus has a lot of followers. The blockbuster movie *Transformers 2* attracted tons of people, and it was a terrible movie. Our goal is NOT a crowd.

Transformation will take place when the age-old principles of spiritual habits are taught and incorporated into someone's life.

Every year we have devoted at least two different five-week sermon series to teaching CORE biblical theological issues. They manifest themselves in different ways. My favorite one is when we teach about our DNA. Our DNA is who we are as a church and what we stand for. It is entirely based on deep theological convictions. It is one of the deepest teachings we do, but it is powerful for new and old believers.

Every year we have also devoted at least two different sermon series on going through a book of the Bible.

One year we only had time for the book of John, but for the most part we have time to dive into two books. We try to do one from the Old Testament and one from the New Testament. This allows us to teach a spiritual habit of how to study the Bible on your own in a large group setting, and it forces us to deal with everything the Bible has to say. There are times we have to discuss and teach some pretty weighty stuff. Like explaining *the Logos* in John's gospel, or divorce, or God's view on sexual sins. When you study a book and not just pick topics, it makes us deal with everything, even when we don't want to!

We also have found that we need to devote times in our annual schedule to teach about softer topics for those who are just getting into the pool. It helps show that we are real people with the same thoughts and issues as everyone else, but a nice way to adjust to the relational climate before diving into deep theological ideas.

### Giving . . . Teach This Now!

Here is one of the biggest problems I am seeing in new churches and their teachings. Most of these church-plants are shying away from teaching about giving.

Almost every church planter who has been around for at least five years will tell you that if they could go back and do it over they would have taught about money earlier than they did and would have brought it up more.

Here is the deal: we church planters know that there are these preconceived ideas of churches that exist in the minds of those who are not followers of Jesus or those who were part of harmful churches at one time. One of those preconceived ideas is that the church is all about money.

It is a legitimate concern. But if you don't address this preconceived idea, then it will stay a preconceived idea.

When you eventually do talk about giving, then there will be people in your new Jesus community who will feel like you pulled a "bait and switch" on them. You will play into their pre-conceived understanding of the church.

DESTROY that idea before they have a chance to ground it into a fact. It isn't *if* you talk about money. It isn't about *when* either. It is more about HOW. If you teach about giving in the right heart, then people will get it. If you beg for money, if you tell them that the church will fold without their money, if you tell them they are financially responsible for the church, then they will not learn to be generous givers. If they give at all, it will be done out of obligation or guilt.

Teach them to be givers. Teach them to be generous.

If you teach this early on, then this spiritual act of worship will not be something the church will struggle with over time.

A pastor called me not long ago to tell me about a church planter he was mentoring and coaching. It appeared that this church planter was struggling with paying the bills of the church, specifically the rent on the facility they were meeting in. This new church was experiencing growth, newfound life in Jesus for those that at one time were not following Him, and seeing positives. The money they had raised at the onset had run out after the first year, and now they were broke.

My pastor friend was at a loss. "I've asked him how many times in the past year has the new church taught about giving, financial generosity, and tithing through sermons and in small groups? This church planter told me ONCE."

Wow!

I was shocked. Shocked because I wasn't expecting this to come from this church planter. Sure, his church was an already cautious cultural crowd, but he didn't seem like the type that would shy away from dealing with issues that are not so fun to talk about.

I asked him why he wasn't teaching about these things and his response to me was, "They know I get paid by the church; I don't want them to think I am teaching about this for my gain."

The sad thing is if he doesn't figure out something soon, then he will need to find another way to make an income, and the church will need to find other ways to hold larger gatherings.

After a few brainstorming ideas with my pastor friend on the phone, we finally came up with a good idea we felt we could present to this church planter. Bring in others to teach on this principle now, and then he could follow up with it every two months until they started to see a difference in maturity in this department.

It worked. In fact, it worked so well that we started doing it at our church.

My friends have made fun of me for bringing others in to speak about tithing and/or giving, but I don't care what they think. It works for us. Once a year, we bring in one of our elders who is outside our church or a great teaching pastor to speak on the subject of tithing and giving. We then make sure we teach about it in our large gatherings at least two other times, that it is part of our one-on-one discipleship, and we offer Dave Ramsey's *Financial Peace University* class twice a year. It is working for us. Those followers of Jesus who call Elevation their home church are learning the spiritual act of worship as it relates to giving.

Side note: I have a lot of church planters who will ask me what is a healthy income for their size of church-plant. There are too many variables for me to offer an exact equation.

A good rule of thumb is that roughly $1,000 per person per year should be given in tithes/offering to the church. So, if there were

100 people that call your Jesus community their home church, then you would see roughly $100,000 income from their giving. Of course, as stated above, this is just a general rule of thumb. How many of those 100 are kids, married, in the prime earning stages of their life, urban dwellers, suburban, rural, white collar, blue collar, college students, etc.? All of it will make the income numbers flux.

Let me say this, though, in regards to income. If you model, teach, and openly discuss giving, you will see your people give not only to further the mission of the Jesus community but to give to God out of worship. The great thing is that usually someone who is doing these things is leading the church in healthy financial decisions and not abusing the giving of the people of Jesus.

If we are going to grow disciples, we must teach people what it means to be a disciple. We can't edit the parts of Scripture that may make us uncomfortable. We must teach all of the scripture. I strongly encourage you to take a look at your teaching plan for the current year, as well as what you did in previous years, to determine whether you have represented a balanced view of what it means to be a disciple or if you have simply spoken on your favorite subjects. Following Jesus is not a choose-your-own-adventure story—it's all or nothing.

# Chapter Nine in Review

*Key Ideas*

1. Church planters must assume that people know little about the Bible.
2. The role of the church is to equip believers, not collect them.
3. Crowds are not a sign of spiritual health.
4. Believers must be taught to feed themselves spiritually.
5. Churches must teach about money early and often.


*Discussion Questions*

1. How should a small group leader focused on teaching new believers respond when a more seasoned believer says the group is too shallow?
2. How can you prevent small groups from being used as a place for marginal believers to hide out and stay for a long time? What would be the consequences of reassigning small groups after 18 months to two years?
3. If crowds are not a sign of spiritual health, why do so many church leaders (and church magazines) celebrate churches with large attendance? How can a new church avoid the trap of measuring success by the size of the crowd?
4. What is your strategy for teaching your congregation to feed themselves spiritually? Why is this so important?
5. Why should the church teach about money regularly?


*Next Steps*

1. Clearly articulate the purpose of small groups.

2. Develop a strategy for attaching small group participation to service in and through the church.
3. Clearly define how your church will measure success.
4. Enlist an adult education specialist to help your church develop a process for teaching believers how to study God's Word.
5. Plan to address the issue of money.

# CHAPTER 10

# BEWARE OF THE PEEING PASTORS

*"This is the kingdom of God, not a kingdom of earthly leaders."*

This is the elephant in the room in most church-planting networks and denominations. It caught me off guard from the very beginning.

I was naïve to the political world of pastor relations within denominations and networks. It hit me hard at the very first meeting I ever had with local pastors before we officially planted.

My fellowship and church-planting network had local rules to planting a new church. One of those rules was that I was to meet with an area leader and two of his committeemen to get permission to plant a church. Knowing all I know now about church planting and the help I have given to all the church-plants I have taught, consulted, and trained, I can now say that this is a little backward.

Their decision to allow me to plant a church was subjective, based on their relationship with me and no other criteria. If you were in tight with these guys, you would have no problem getting permission to plant a church whether you were qualified or called to do so. It wasn't that these guys were bad men; they were just operating in a system that was flawed.

Here I was sitting at this meeting thinking this was going to be easy. I knew God called me. I was trained. I had assessed very high for being a successful church planter. I had two church ministry positions under my belt as experience. I had the support from my national and regional religious leaders to plant a church. This wasn't supposed to be as hard as it turned out to be.

I was peppered with questions. One launched right after another. I am sure if these men were to recall the meeting, they probably wouldn't remember it the same way, because I was more caught off guard than I let on. The questions had nothing to do with my calling from God. The questions all had to do with my planned relational connections with other churches of our fellowship and network.

Who was I going to get to help me plant the church? What would I do if someone from another one of our fellowship churches came to my church? How would I raise money from our fellowship churches? How far away would our church be from other fellowship churches? Since I was leaving one of our fellowship churches, what was my plan for continued relationships with those I once pastored?

Then the biggest question of all.

"If we say no, what will you do?"

That was a loaded question.

Whether they intended it to be or not, this question put all the weight on my relationship with local pastors (them).

"Well, I would respectfully listen to the decision you made and why you made that decision. I would take it into consideration and work with my mentors to evaluate the best move to make after that, but I would have to be honest and tell you that this is a calling from God and I will plant a church no matter what."

It wasn't what they were looking for. One of them looked okay with my answer, probably because he didn't ask the question. The other two just stared at me and finally dismissed me from the meeting.

They eventually notified me that they approved us to plant a church, but I didn't learn from this experience the way I should have.

### The Problem with Pastors

I didn't realize how important my relationships were with other pastors in the area. Back then I had no clue that there are certain rules we seem to live by in the "pastor circles." I am guessing—and I am telling you this is a complete guess—that these rules came from the days when 80 percent of the United States citizens were church attenders and you were basically trying to convince people to jump denominations and not just accept Jesus into their lives.

For instance, I made a huge mistake with this on month three of our new church-plant. I wrote letters to members of my former church where I served as associate pastor, asking them for help. Now, I sent these form letters to a ton of different people across America who were on my database, including the names of those from my former church who I was super close to, had a heart for prayer, were itching to go out on a ministry adventure, and had the financial means to help us. I actually had people on my database from my last TWO churches.

I got in trouble for this.

Before I knew it, the pastor of one of the churches sent a letter to my regional leadership telling them I was unethical, was stealing people from his church, and I was violating the commitment I had made to him in leaving to plant this church.

Now, I don't agree with this pastor, but what I learned made me realize I had made a mistake.

Benny Hinn asks for money every day from people from all different churches, and they give. I haven't seen or heard of anyone writing him letters asking him to stop or telling him it is unethical. Okay, overblown example. I get it.

The unwritten rule is that people who attend a church are not to be contacted by leaders from other churches without consent from that person's current church leadership. I don't care if you like it or not, but pew protectors hold to this unwritten rule.

Here is the mistake I made and the rule that existed within these "pastor circles." I hadn't asked for consent. I probably could have written the same letters to the people from that church had I asked permission from their pastor. I eventually had to write a retraction letter. I didn't mind apologizing, because I honestly had no clue it was going to cause such heartache for this pastor. My intention wasn't to harm him personally, so I wanted to do all I could to remedy this situation.

In the meeting where I apologized and we came to an agreement on me writing retraction letters, I saw my second glimpse into pastor relations.

This pastor wanted me to report back to him every time I talked to someone from his church. So, if I ran into them at the grocery store, saw them at a concert, or they contacted me; I was to report back to him. Now, his church is roughly twenty minutes from where we were planting and over two hundred thousand people lived in between our two churches. Two hundred thousand, and 3 percent of them were evangelical Christians. Lesson learned: pastors are nervous about losing people from their congregations.

I wondered why this fear existed. It certainly never crossed my mind.

### Pew Protectors vs. Team Players

Whether we like it or not, there are two types of pastors we will encounter when we plant new Jesus communities: Team Players and Pew Protectors.

Pew protectors don't understand discipleship and build their churches mainly by attracting or keeping existing followers of Jesus. They usually don't experience growth, and if they do it is all transfer growth. They have lost the spark of life that comes from seeing people come to Jesus for the first time and discipleship taking place.

They live off of the "good ol' days." All their stories are of the past, and they have no vision for the future. They are not bad men or women; they have just forgotten what this Jesus stuff is all about. Like a dog that pees on a fire hydrant to mark its territory, these leaders haven't learned that it isn't about gathering a quantity or area to stake a claim.

If people are something to be entertained or they left one church to come to yours, then you should be worried if another church-plant comes into your area. They might entertain them better or they will leave your church as they did when they left their previous church to come to yours.

But if it is about equipping the saints for the ministry, the ministry being discipleship, then people live and work to be on mission with Jesus and not to be consumers. They don't need another church to come into the area, but if a new church does, they celebrate over more workers available to gather the harvest.

When I would talk about this with other leaders they would tell me that these pastors are insecure. I have pondered this for years now, and I don't think that insecurity is the issue. Insecurity is the issue if our job is to get people to follow us, love us, and the church is an extension of who we are as leaders. If that is the case, then I understand insecurity being something we deal with as leaders. It isn't the reason we have churches.

This is the kingdom of God, not a kingdom of earthly leaders.

Remember this principle: We are not IT, we are just part of IT. Christian churches share the gospel in common.

It just manifests itself in a thousand different ways. Each one might give emphasis to areas that are not necessarily areas you feel deserve to be highlighted, but you will never know what God has asked them to be. You can only worry about what God has asked you to be.

People will come and go. Some will be consumers who are looking for the next shiny trinket. Remember what you were called to do: make disciples and build the kingdom of God—not organize a 501(c)3.

## How to Deal with Pew Protectors

You will encounter them. Some will try to run you off. They will do everything possible to stop you. I wish I was kidding when I say this, but we actually had churches in our area where the pastors got up on Sunday mornings and told their congregations that our new church didn't preach from the Bible, didn't do worship, did an hour of worship, or that I cussed during my sermons. The rumors were flying in the pew protectors' churches. I didn't take it personal because I realized that they forgot the point of all we do is Jesus.

I am sure that you can add more things to this list, but I sure wish someone had talked to me about this before I planted. Here are a few suggestions on how to deal with this *when* the time and situation arises:

*1. Ignore what needs to be ignored.*

Who cares if someone says you don't preach the Bible to a bunch of people who are already "saved"? That isn't who you are trying to reach anyways, right? God didn't call you to take people from other churches. Ignore it. My big rule of thumb is this: if you make it a big deal, it will be a big deal.

If a pastor is upset and complaining, evaluate the situation and decide if it is worth addressing. Most of the time it is not. If you have actually done something that has hurt a relationship with them, then apologize and move on, but don't play into the complaining game of others.

Let your default reaction be to IGNORE.

*2. Play nice.*

It is super easy to react to others the way they are treating you. Don't do it. I am guilty of not following this rule. A local pastor called my fellowship regional director to complain when he found out that we had a house church in his area. He was upset and told them that I never got permission from him to have a house church nearby. Not too long after this I was at a local pastors meeting, and he was there. We happened to be assigned to sit by each other and discuss a particular issue. I was not nice in my responses to him. I was not playing nice and was treating him as I felt he was treating me, but that isn't right.

*3. Turn the other cheek (someone really smart said that once).*

Don't react with a slap for a slap. Kill them with kindness when they are being mean to you or complaining about you. This is a Jesus principle more than it is anything else, and it is the heart of God. He doesn't want us to fight with each other. They might have a crazy view of what is going on around them, but it shouldn't change our view of being loving and kind toward them. It will be hard to be anything but mean to them, but forgive them and love them.

*4. Honor what needs to be honored.*

This is one of the principles you use with your kids. Praise good behavior. Same thing goes for the pew protectors in your area. If you shower them with honor in areas that need honoring, you reinforce behavior. Hopefully, this will lead to you seeing more behavior that is kingdom-minded.

A pew protector in our area who had given us nothing but grief eventually decided to plant a church. I am being generous with that term here; as what happened is that a bunch of people from their church left and wanted to do their own thing. The pew protector decided not to fight it, and publicly got behind the new endeavor. We saw this public action and we praised, honored, and celebrated this pastor for his new church-plant. Great thing is, he is actually now helping to get more church-plants in the area. People like to be praised and recognized. If you recognize the good qualities of these pew protectors, you will cultivate good behavior.

*5. Bite your tongue.*

There is no need to speak out against these pastors.

None.

It will not bring forth anything good in the kingdom of God. You will want to blog about them, you will want to use them as illustrations in your sermons, you will want to talk to other pastors about them. Don't do it. Bite your tongue.

There was one pastor who, in the middle of his Sunday morning sermon, would call out our church by name and say, "I don't like that church over there—that Elevation Church."

My phone was ringing off the hook from people asking me if I had heard what this pastor had said. I played it off to all those who called me, ignoring their comments and remarks. I was flustered inside. I immediately went online to listen to this sermon. Yep, sure enough, what everyone had told me was true. Our leaders started to buzz about it and finally asked me, "What are we going to do about this?"

I went to God in prayer. I was hurt that another Christian church would not like us or say negative things about us. I prayed to God to understand how we should respond.

I decided that starting the next Sunday, we would pray for a different local church in our area each week. If others wanted to bash, we were going to pray for unity. And so even now, every Sunday at Elevation Church we pray for a different local Christian church. We want to bite our tongues to the negative things we could say and speak words of praise, blessing, and honor over fellow churches.

Control your tongue even when you seem to have all the right in the world to unleash its power.

*6. Be a team player.*

Team players understand that we are all on the same team for Jesus. They are not worried about making a name for themselves or their churches. A desire to see people find Jesus and grow in their understanding of Jesus propels them in ministry. There is nothing more energizing than being around other pastors and leaders who have a heart for God's kingdom and not their own.

Team players want to know what is going on with your church community and family life. They don't care to tell you about themselves, they care about others first. Team players want to be involved with helping you succeed as a church and will seek out ways to be united. Team players praise church-plants and pray for more of them. Team players prioritize meeting with other team players.

I recommend hanging out with team players on a regular basis. Maybe meeting once a month or every other month. Keeping yourself involved relationally with these types of leaders will keep your focus on church as a kingdom sport and not an empire for you to build. We are all bit players in this grand epic; get to know the rest of the cast.

I know your time will be swamped. You will probably have to rearrange your schedule, but you need to spend time with like-minded leaders in your area. We will move heaven and earth for what we care about; this is something TO care about.

There is a group of church leaders in my area that gets together for prayer, golf, book discussions, unity events, etc. These leaders are all team players. I love being with them. I am on the road a lot, so I don't get to hang with them as much as I want, but when I am in town I make a point to spend time with them. I want to be connected to those who will build me and the Jesus community I am part of UP . . . there are plenty of people out there trying to pull us down.

In the same way that we honor the pew protectors for their good behavior, I suggest honoring team players as well. Bless them. Love them. Show them you are on their team as much as they are on yours. This might come in many different forms: doing a local missions trip to help their church with a building or cleanup project, giving gifts, bringing them to your church and praying for them, inviting their pastors to speak at your church, joining with them on a mission trip or promoting an outreach or event in your community, etc.

A church that was pastored by one of the best team players I know would have a big missions convention every year. Part of the convention was a missions banquet for all of their people to attend. It was a nice dinner at a hotel conference center. I would try to honor and bless them by taking twenty to thirty youth with me to babysit their kids at the church building so that none of their people had to miss out on the banquet. We would spend three plus hours playing with their kids, eating pizza, and watching movies. It was awesome. Invest in the local team players, and be creative about how you can help them out.

Working WITH the local team players is another way you keep up your relationship with them. We have done Good Friday services with other churches, Christmas events, parties, worship events, youth camps, mission trips, mission outreaches, etc. It just seems obvious to me that if you believe you are all on the same team, then act like it! You can put that into action right away. We have several sister churches in our area because of the relationships I have built with their leaders and through us working together. There is nothing that communicates better than this.

*7. Welcome new churches in your area.*

I think the last suggestion I could give you in the relationships department for your interaction with team player leaders is that when new church-plants come into your area, be the first to welcome them to the neighborhood. Treat them as you would have wanted others to treat you.

Even this morning, before I began to write this chapter, I sent off an e-mail to a new church-plant leader. I welcomed him to Utah and asked if there was anything we could do to help them get off to a good start. Of course I invited him to coffee as well, but that is a given with me. Coffee always makes good relationships.

Your church-plant has the ability, even in the infant stages, to connect with other church-plants. Develop a kingdom heart in you and your leadership from day one, and when day three thousand hits, you will be writing the book on local relationships with other churches.

# Chapter Ten in Review

*Key Ideas*

1. Relationships with other church leaders are vital.
2. Some leaders of nearby churches will not be supportive of your efforts to start a new church.
3. Church planters must learn to ignore what needs to be ignored and honor what needs to be honored.
4. Church planters recognize their role as part of the team with neighboring churches.
5. A kingdom heart always celebrates the kingdom's advance.

*Discussion Questions*

1. How can you develop relationships with other church leaders?
2. What will you do when you discover that a neighboring pastor is more discouraging than supporting?
3. What are three things you can do to honor other church leaders in your community?
4. How can you invest in or partner with the ministries of other nearby churches?
5. Which nearby church leader do you think is most likely to celebrate your church's success with you?

*Next Steps*

1. Plan to have lunch or coffee with neighboring pastors.
2. Be prepared to respond to those who are discouraging to you.
3. Identify the church leaders you need to ignore and those you can celebrate with.

4. List some ways you can partner with a local church to support its ministry and build a positive relationship.
5. Invite a neighboring church leader to serve as a mentor or advisor.

# CHAPTER 11

# GET YOUR FAT BUTT TO THE GYM

*"If you don't love yourself and worry about yourself, you will be the sacrifice in the church-planting process."*

All the research will tell you that pastoring has become an unhealthy profession emotionally and physically. (I'll explain this more as you keep reading.)

I believe church planting CAN be one thousand times worse.

I have always been a relatively healthy chap. My weight has always been right within what is expected of my height, weight, and age.

I played sports throughout high school and the first year of college, so I was very conscious of my eating habits. In fact, I didn't drink carbonated drinks or soda for most of high school and all of college. Working out every week, if not every day, wasn't a chore. That was just life.

It almost seemed as if the day we said yes to church planting our health graph was starting to decline. I lost almost twenty pounds in the first two months of working on the church-plant. The stress of working on it was keeping me awake at night. Eating just wasn't appealing at all.

I remember one such occasion of sitting down to eat my favorite food, sushi, while I was traveling and speaking about our new church-plant at a church on the east coast. While I was sitting there I ordered what I would consider my usual consumption. The order came to the table and I ate three pieces of sushi. That was it.

Done.

I couldn't eat any more.

My eating habits seemed to mirror my wife's when she was pregnant. I left the sushi place perplexed. It dawned on me at that moment, I wasn't eating anymore.

That was the first year of church planting. Before I knew it, my eating and weight went in the opposite direction. I was eating twice the amount I normally would eat and I gained almost forty pounds in a matter of six months.

That was just the physical side.

The stress was killing me.

I am a hard worker and have a great work ethic that I developed from my father. I don't ever stop working, really. It has never been a problem in my life because I knew when to relax. But it was as if church planting didn't ever allow me to stop and relax.

In the first three years of planting the church, I didn't use any vacation days.

I was constantly dealing with one issue after the next, though not begrudgingly; I just worked hard at being the best pastor I could be. In my mind, that meant making sure I handled everything swiftly.

Finally, it hit me.

One day of not feeling like a champ turned into two days.
Two days turned into five days.
Five days turned into two weeks.

What was going on with me? All I wanted to do was nap, and I didn't have any passion left in my tank.

### Someone Noticed What I Ignored

One of the deacons at my church noticed my mood had changed. I was impressed because socially I was the Tom Cruise of church planting, acting as if everything was awesome inside. I lived on energy drinks to get me through having to be around large crowds of people. He pulled me aside, and I confessed that I wasn't me inside. I had no idea what to do about it. The typical Christian methods of dealing with these things were not working: fasting, praying, digestion of the Word of God, more prayer, etc. Nothing was helping. I wanted to crawl into a cave and hibernate forever.

My dear deacon friend confessed that he was suffering from depression and had been on anti-depressants. Oh great, that is the last thing I need to be on. What will people think if I am taking a drug to help me out emotionally?

He gave me the name of a doctor, and off I went to schedule my appointment.

The day I walked into the doctor's office was really a miracle from God. When the doctor walked into the room, I introduced myself. He kindly responded, "I know who you are; I go to your church."

Okay. Great. Even better. (Sarcasm here.)

I told him everything I was feeling, and they ran tests on me. The tests came back that I was mildly hypoglycemic. He explained to me about how our bodies produce emotions via the chemicals in our brains, which vitamins supply those chemicals, and what I can do to help my body stay on track to function properly. Then he prayed with me. His nurse even prayed with me when she was taking my blood.

Here I was, a guy who was supposed to be this mighty church planter, sitting in a doctor's office depressed, physically unhealthy, with the doctor and his staff praying for me. What is going on? Seems I should be praying for them.

My doctor prescribed anti-depressants. And, you know what, after looking at my diet, physical health, and days off . . . the medication helped.

I was back.

There are a lot of "I's" in this story for me. I felt that it was my fault entirely. I had screwed up. I had done something wrong. I was broken.

This wasn't just an "I" or "me" problem. This is a "we" problem.

Pain is the body's way of letting us know something is wrong. Both physical and emotional pain. None of us like pain, but it is necessary to have in our life so that it will draw attention to something we need to take care of.

Guilt, for instance, is a great emotional pain. Without it, how would we know that we needed to humble ourselves, repent, make things right, and move back to God?

Everything I was experiencing from the physical to the emotional was letting me know something was wrong, not because I was a bad, messed up person or because I had done something or allowed a decision to hurt me. My body was drawing attention to the fact that something was wrong, and it needed attention.

We (and by *we* I mean us pastors and church planters) are in a realm of work that is unhealthy both physically and emotionally. If we are not careful, our bodies will let us know with pain when we have neglected to protect ourselves from the unhealthy ramifications of our job.

Now, I know that some of you are sitting there going, "What? Our job isn't unhealthy!" But it is.

In August of 2010, Paul Vitello wrote an article published in the *New York Times* with the title "Taking a Break from the Lord's Work." The reason he wrote this article was articulated in the second sentence of the article, "Members of the clergy now suffer from obesity, hypertension and depression at rates higher than most Americans."

The article went on to recount the research that has been done on clergy and their health, both physical and emotional. All of the research has pointed to the fact that we, as pastors, are unhealthy as a result of our jobs.

There are no simple explanations to sum it all up. Reading the article and diving into the research that was done by Duke University and other groups helped me to understand myself more in the context of the unhealthy behaviors I allowed the job of church planting to attach to my life.

### Never Stopping

Whether it was a sense of duty from God to answer every phone call or e-mail, whether it was the hard work that was instilled in me from my father, I never stopped. Most church planters don't!

My wife and I had lunch with a church planter and his wife recently, and his wife said to us, "Oh, he works two full-time jobs. forty hours at his job that he gets paid for and sixty hours at the church-plant."

God's insistence on a Sabbath starts in Genesis, the beginning, when our God takes a Sabbath. Not a holy day, not a day of religious obligation, but a day of REST.

Smarter people than I have taught on this idea of the Sabbath, and there are great books to read on this topic. The bottom line is that you and I were not made to WORK 24/7. We are not machines. This world does not hinge on our work. We are only small players in a grand epic, God has this thing in control, and His will will be done. If you take one day a week to REST, it will not fall apart.

I had to learn to turn off my phone on my day off. I had to learn to stop checking my e-mail on my day off. I had to learn that when my Sabbath came, even if my work was not finished, my work was finished.

I remember that the first time I started to implement this in my life, I saw what I thought was a train wreck happening before my eyes.

My Sabbath is Fridays, my day of rest. I was working with our marketing company on mass mailers for one of our new campuses. The mass mailer was to let everyone in our community know of the new location and public gatherings. We were up against a deadline. If we didn't close on the deal with our art, payment, etc., by that Friday, we couldn't hit the dates we wanted with the mass mailers. Thursday came and went, and for a lot of different circumstances we were unable to finish the project.

Friday came.

I itched to get on the phone, check my e-mail, and finish the project. Something inside of me (okay, it was God) said NO. This is your day to rest. My work was finished even when my work wasn't finished.

You know what? Everything worked out.

You can always find an excuse on why you need to work on your day off. Something can always be labeled important. If you start making exceptions, you will never stop.

It isn't just Sabbaths, or rest days, that you and I neglect in our church planting jobs. We don't take vacations either. I bragged about it to my leaders once to show my dedication to the church-plant, "I haven't taken a vacation day in three years." Now, when I hear that I want to slap someone. That is not healthy! You need time away, you need extended periods of time *not* working, and it is vital.

Due to the research that has been conducted on clergy health, some denominations are now requiring vacation days to be used no matter what; they are even scheduling it out for their clergy who will not do it themselves. Some are even requiring sabbaticals to be taken after so many years of full-time pastoral work.

I think it goes to a deeper issue inside of us; we think it all depends on US.

We play a part in the church-plant's success, no doubt. But only to a point. God plays a part the whole way. Live that out in the way you work.

Work hard and rest hard.

## Never Slowing DOWN

You may think I'm still on the topic of not taking time off for rest, but slowing down has to do with the days you *do* work. Our pace of work can be unhealthy. It dawned on me when talking to Ken and Austin Andrews. Ken is the pastor of Pasadena Christian Center in Pasadena, California. Ken and his son, Austin, were contestants on the Biggest Loser season 11. They both experienced major health problems, Ken more than Austin, and both lost almost two hundred pounds each when it was all said and done.

Now, you might think that these guys were just overweight people, but as I listened to them and heard what they had to say, I realized that they were victims of the pastoral lifestyle as I was myself. It just piled up on them over the years, but the manifestations were just more obvious (and public thanks to the show) in their lives.

Austin said to me, "As a part of the on-the-go lifestyle of a ministry family, fast food was a regular part of our life." Ken agreed with Austin, saying that the lifestyle of a pastor has to do with being non-physical in nature, lots of meetings, and most of those meetings being around food.

Slowing down our actual workdays is something we NEED to do. If we don't, we will kill ourselves. We were not built to maintain top speed throughout any given day.

Do you schedule time in your day just to sit and relax?

Do you schedule time in your day where you turn off your e-mail and cell phone?

Do you schedule time in your day for naps?

I found I was happier, physically able to do more, *and* still able to get everything done on time when I slowed down and planned my day with MARGINS. Buffer areas that allowed the day to slow down and allowed me to watch my physical and mental health.

You will feel as I did, that there seems to be urgency all over the place with planting the church. Urgency for the church community as a whole, people with their own urgent needs and requests, etc. Social media and the new telecommunications of the world make getting a message to us pastors easy, and it usually feels as though everything is so urgent.

We create boundary issues in our own lives when we take the urgencies of others and the church community as something we have to fix.

There will always be something urgent to take care of. Trust me on this. Everyday will bring with it a new urgency.

Don't let urgency dictate your day. It will kill you.

Slow down the day. You will find that you complete things with excellence, and you will feel better at the end of the day physically and mentally. Meals should not be missed, and don't allow fast food to become a staple of your diet. SLOW DOWN.

## Never Taking Care of ME

We are trained and conditioned in ministry that it isn't about us. This belief infects our ministry lives so much that it almost seems selfish or counter-intuitive for us pastors to worry about ourselves in addition to the church, our family, and others.

I felt guilty worrying about myself and taking care of my own spiritual, mental, and physical health.

*Was I reading the Bible to feed myself or just to study it to teach others?*
*Was I getting enough sleep at night?*
*Was I going to the gym and giving my body the physical workout and nourishment it needed?*
*Was I reading books to inspire and speak to me, or were they just for WORK?*
*Was I taking alone times to withdraw from the crowds and connect with God?*

Jesus said that the two greatest commandments were loving God and loving others as we love ourselves. The problem with this statement for us church planters is that we are great at loving two out of the three He mentioned in that statement.

We love God. We love others. But we don't really love ourselves.

We give lots of time doing for God, serving God, loving people, serving people, but we don't give equal time to loving ourselves. How sad it is when a church-plant reaches people and worships Jesus only to watch the church planter wither away and die?

One of my best friends planted a church. He was a great communicator, a great leader, and he could attract anyone to follow him into his next vision from God. He was gifted. As the years went on, his fast pace never allowed him to stop, let alone slow down. He neglected himself so much that eventually (and before he knew it) the church was doing great . . . but he wasn't the pastor anymore. Further, he was separated from his wife and kids.

If you don't love yourself and worry about yourself, you will be the sacrifice in the church-planting process. What good is it to gain the whole world and sacrifice your soul?

Take time for you.
Go on a retreat by yourself.
Take days off that are just for you to be you.
Join a gym.
Join a karate class.
Read books that are not about ministry methods.
Schedule time with just you and God.

If you are not fully you, your church-plant can never be fully itself.

**Pay Attention to Your Physical Life**

Join a gym or workout group, do some activity that forces you to be active. As pastors, we do a lot of sitting and eating. Get outside of this realm ON PURPOSE, not by chance.

Pastor Ken, from the *Biggest Loser* season 11, gave me great advice on being active as a pastor, "I have oodles of phone calls to make and return. Instead of sitting at my desk and making them, I now make a list of all the calls and go walking outside. I used to pray on my knees the majority of the time, now I walk the streets around my church building and community. I make appointments at a local coffee shop that is 1.4 miles from my office. I choose to walk rather than drive. The excuses I hear from others, 'Well that works for you, but I live in the country, the closest coffee shop to my house or church [building] is 9 miles.' My answer . . . drive 7.6 miles, park your car, and walk the rest of the way."

### Pay Attention to Your Mental Life

Are you giving yourself enough breaks during the day to decompress? Are you giving yourself breaks throughout the week to just NOT work? Schedule fun things to do that you love doing and go do them!

Take up hobbies.
Read great books.
Read books you WANT to read.
Date your spouse.

Relax and let your mind rest. You are no less of a person by giving your brain time to focus on things other than the church-plant. You need it!

## Pay Attention to Your Spiritual Life

The scariest thing that could happen to us as church planters is we become experts in God and church life, without knowing God personally.

Spend time with God for just you, not for the church community or others—just you.

King David inspires me every time I read the Psalms. He complains to God and praises God and thanks God, but it seems to me that the majority of the time it is about himself personally and not the nation he is king of. That inspires me to keep myself close to God first and foremost.

Last, but not least in all of this talk on what is healthy, love your family well, spend time with them, slow down for them, put them in your schedule, make them part of the life of the church, retreat with them, vacation with them, make them a priority. Not only would it be sad to see a church planter die on the vine of planting, but it would be sadder to see a church planter's family sacrificed too.

## Don't Sacrifice Your Family

I sat around the dining room table one night as we were eating dinner. At the time my daughters were three and five years old. I stopped eating and told the family I was sorry I had neglected them so much because of the pace of life I was living.

My wife started to tear up as she stopped eating to listen to me.

"I am committed to this family and any one of you in this family has the veto power to jump in at anytime and tell me if you don't want me to be pastor anymore because it is harming this family."

My youngest daughter, Berlyn, didn't even look up from her food, "It's okay, Daddy, you can be a pastor."

Madison, my oldest, smiled at me, "Okay, we will let you know."

My family knows they are a priority in my life.

You can plant a church without killing yourself or your family. I promise.

# CHAPTER ELEVEN IN REVIEW

*Key Ideas*

1. Church planting is psychologically and physically taxing.
2. There are some common dangers that church leaders must avoid.
3. Resting is often more important than working harder.
4. The success of a church-plant isn't dependent upon one individual.
5. A church leader must have a plan for exercising his physical, mental, and spiritual life.

*Discussion Questions*

1. What are the psychological dangers associated with church leadership?
2. Which of the common dangers listed in chapter 11 are you most susceptible to? Why? What can you do to protect yourself from those dangers?
3. What is your strategy for resting? How important is resting to your ministry?
4. How are you building a team and what is its role in helping carry the weight of the ministry? Why is this so important?
5. What is your daily plan for exercising physically, mentally, and spiritually?

*Next Steps*

1. Identify a Christian counselor to whom you can turn in times of need.
2. List 3–5 action steps that will help you combat the dangers listed in this chapter.

3. Set aside time in your weekly schedule for rest and relaxation.

4. Invest weekly in those 2–3 key leaders that are most critical to the establishment of the church.

5. Schedule time in your weekly schedule to exercise three times. Also schedule mental breaks and time to focus on your personal spiritual health.

# CHAPTER 12

# JESUS, THANK YOU FOR LETTING ME SEE THIS

*"We get to be on the front lines of this grand epic,
living out the mission, discipling others, and teaching them
to live as Jesus taught us to live."*

In the end, if you follow what God is asking you to do and disciple others, you will see God grow His bride, the church, in ways you will never understand.

Bob Roberts Jr. tweeted that we should worry about growing the church big and not growing big churches.

Planting a church is almost like a rebirth of your Christianity.

Prayers seem exciting as when you first became a follower of Jesus. I know Jesus was answering my prayers before, but He was answering more because I was praying a lot more during the church-plant than I was before. There was something about it. Anticipation of an answer lived in every prayer and lingered in each thought throughout the day.

Fasting feels energized and powerful. I have never fasted more than in my days of first planting our church. I was so eager for God to reach people through us; I was willing to give up my comfort to focus on God's heart. It wasn't agonizing; it was exciting to see God speak and guide.

You spend more time on your knees praying for God's presence and favor. The joke I tell other church planters is that they need to buy kneepads before they ever set off to plant a church. You will be on your knees more than you have ever been in your life. It will feel like begging, pleading, rejoicing, exalting, asking, listening, etc.

And you regain your perspective on caring to see God bring in the harvest, the fruit.

The fruit of church planting is changed lives. Growing the kingdom of God bigger. This fruit will be lasting fruit. It will be worth every anxiety, every worry, every stress, every late night, every counseling session, every troubled church attendee, and every problem.

The days come when I am down and out. The days come when I ask, "what am I doing?" The days come when I feel like I am spinning my wheels, but all I have to do is remember the fruit—and remember them by name . . .

### Jenny

Even though Jenny grew up in Utah, she didn't grow up in the dominant religion. She grew up in the World Wide Church of God. The rules of the World Wide Church were extreme compared to those she lived around. Jenny and her five other siblings lived a life of strict devotion to these rules.

For whatever reason (maybe the rules of the church or her relationship with her dad), Jenny was eager to get out of the house at eighteen and get far away from the life she grew up in.

She searched for love and acceptance in her new world away from her past life. It wasn't hard to find for Jenny. Her bright smile and contagious personality were very easy attractions to those she encountered. Before she knew it, a boy was in her life who she thought would save her from all that was wrong in the world.

The problem was that this boy was toxic. Abusive, both physically and mentally, to her. He controlled her life with an iron fist. Holding her down and screaming in her face if she didn't follow his lead. He manipulated her, isolated her, and would remind her everyday that she was worthless without him. Somehow she was able to muster up the courage to get out of this relationship. Leave all behind again and move on.

She didn't want to be alone during this new time in her life, but she didn't have anyone to comfort her through the pain of her past relationship, and she was lonely. She found this comfort in the arms of another woman. In Jenny's own words, she says, "I was running away from everything and seeking some sense of control and the complete opposite of everything I had known in my previous relationship."

They moved in together and started making plans for their future together. This was a safe relationship for her to be in. She was in control, unlike the last relationship, and there was nothing abusive in her new companion.

Something wasn't right, though.

Something in her was aching for something more.

She hadn't found it in following rules from her childhood, she hadn't found it in following rules from her abusive boyfriend, she hadn't found it from her girlfriend. In fact, she hadn't found it anywhere.

Searching for this THING, this thing she had no clue what it was . . .

By the time her father passed away, Jenny's mom had left the World Wide Church of God. Mom was now going to a Jesus-following church and realizing the grace and mercy of God.

Jenny started attending these services with her mom and almost immediately she could sense God as she walked into the service. Here is what she had been searching for her whole life. She had found it. She didn't know how to take it home with her, so for her it was just something she could experience in a service.

Her girlfriend confronted her one day saying, "I feel like the closer you get to this Jesus, the farther you get from me."

It was true.

Jenny made the decision to move out and follow after God with all that was inside of her. She lost everything. Her girlfriend changed the locks on the house and wouldn't give her any of her possessions.

"Who cares? I got Jesus!"

Two years later, Jenny joined our staff. Taking over the hospitality ministry of our church, helping to lead the women's ministry, and sharing her story of healing with college students all over the western states.

Marrying another church leader after healing from the pains of relationships past, Jenny is a walking example of God's healing power.

Jesus, thank You for letting me see this.

### Becky

Every week for almost two years, our church planting team would meet at this local dive of a restaurant for a Tuesday morning breakfast and meeting. Sometimes a few of us would go and study the Bible together at breakfast later during the week as well.

We decided to pick a server and always sit in her section. That way we would get to know her and build a good relationship. Our server we picked was a nice girl who didn't smile much but was always willing to help us out when we were there. A single mom with a work ethic that would rival anyone's, this girl was determined to make a life for her and her daughter.

Becky became OUR server. She would even have our table ready with coffee when we would show up on Tuesdays. And if for some reason we didn't show up one week, we would hear about it the next.

We tipped her well. We treated her with respect. We considered her our friend.

One early morning breakfast as I sat there with our worship leader studying the book of Acts, Becky came to pour our coffee. "You guys part of a church or something?"

"Yes, we are."

"Why haven't you invited me?"

Wow! She was ready. I wanted to be sarcastic and respond back, "Because you wouldn't have come until we had built this relationship with you, but now you will."

We invited her to the opening of our new location on Easter and she was there, crying on the third row throughout the whole worship service. She prayed with one of our female leaders to accept God into her life and she was there every week.

Jesus, thank You for letting me see this.

### Sam and Debbie

My co-pastor, Ryan, moved into his new house in Utah the same day I moved into mine. I wasn't able to help him move in but was at his house almost every week. He lived in a great little neighborhood roughly one mile away from the Salt Lake. The type where every neighbor knows each other.

One afternoon, one of the neighbors decided to bring some leftover fruits from their fruit garden around to the rest of the neighbors. Debbie knocked on Ryan's door and his wife, Molly, answered. Molly struck up a conversation and before you knew it they were neighbor-friends.

Debbie's husband, Sam, was brought in on the new neighborhood friendship and soon all four of them were hanging out for dinners. At one of these dinners the conversation came up of why Ryan and Molly had moved to Utah of all places.

Ryan explained how they had moved to Utah to plant a church. A foreign concept for anyone that would call Utah home, this wasn't something that was easy to understand for Sam and Debbie. Why was Ryan home all the time? How does one "plant a church"? Ryan told his new friends the launch date for the Sunday services and how we would be renting a movie theater to hold our public gatherings. This meant lots of preparation on Sunday mornings and lots of setup since it wasn't our building.

Sam and Debbie both had been born and raised in Utah. Debbie came from a Mormon background, and Sam didn't have any church history. They didn't know much about church, but they offered to watch Ryan and Molly's kids on Sunday mornings so they didn't have to get up and leave so early with their parents to do the setup. They also offered to take the kids to church and attend the first service, at Ryan's request that they check it out and give some honest feedback, no strings attached to ever come back again.

In Debbie's own words, she said, "We only planned to attend the first service, and we haven't left since."

Before you knew it Debbie and Sam had given their lives to Jesus. At our first baptism service they were both baptized by Ryan into Christ.

Ryan bought Sam a Christmas gift that year. A brand-new Bible, with the inscription "Use it wisely, thanks for being our neighbor and friend and we appreciate you and your family."

As Sam opened the gift, tears fell from his eyes. It was the first Bible he had ever owned. "This is the best gift anyone could have given me," Sam said.

Jesus, thank You for letting me see this.

## Dustin

Dustin showed up to our first Sunday gathering at the movie theater. He was invited by the sister of one of the band members. Dustin was a single dad who was down and out in life. No real hope, no real community to belong to, and just trying to make it through each day.

As the band began to play and worship flowed from the audience, Dustin was overwhelmed with the presence of God. Tears fell from his eyes, and he couldn't stop crying through the service.

He was introduced to the band after the service, as Dustin was a bass player and musician himself. Instantly our band connected with him and invited him to play on the team. They were looking for a bass player, and he accepted the invitation with complete joy and dedication.

He was at every practice. He was at every service.

He played his heart out for God.

Before you knew it, as our first baptism approached, Dustin was the first one asking to be dunked for Jesus.

It was an honor to baptize Dustin at our first baptism. This once-depressed and somber man was now full of life and happiness for God.

Just a few years later, Dustin would meet the woman of his dreams.

### Mandy

Dustin started bringing Mandy with him to Sunday gatherings and teaching her about Jesus. We could all see that they were perfect for each other and they were following after Jesus together. Mandy was also a single parent, with three amazing kids. She was always smiling and thought the world of Dustin.

Dustin baptized Mandy at our summer baptism party. And they made plans for a future together.

They were married not long after with most of those in attendance being his new church community friends and family. Their lives were being transformed.

A year later, Dustin was diagnosed with cancer.

As despair would haunt almost anyone in this situation, it didn't faze Dustin. "I know where I am going if this doesn't end well for me."

Less than a year later, Dustin passed on to be with Jesus.

I could talk about how much Dustin touched all of us who knew him or how he grew in Jesus in such a short time, but his real legacy was established at the baptism party two months after Dustin's funeral. His step-son was baptized because of what Dustin had shown him—Jesus.

Here we had seen Dustin baptized, his wife baptized by Dustin, and now his wife baptizing their son.

Jesus, thank You for letting me see this.

### Mike

I had only met Mike a handful of times. He was married just recently to one of our volunteers. I didn't know much about Mike other than he was in upper management with his company and had been married before with grown kids.

It was a few weeks after Easter that I got a message from Mike via e-mail. We needed to meet up, so we headed to my favorite hangout, Starbucks. I had no clue what he wanted to talk about, so this was going to be interesting. There he was sitting at a table with a coffee when I got there. His wife had sent me a text to bring a Bible with me to our meeting. I handed him the Bible and sat down across from him.

"I wanted to meet with you because I need to make a decision."

"Okay. What's going on?"

"I went to your Easter service, and it was different than any other time I have been. Something hit me, and I know it was God. I need to decide if I am going to follow the faith of my youth or follow your Jesus. Will you please teach me about Jesus?"

That meeting started a series of meetings that is actually still going on to this day. Every week at Starbucks, Mike and I meet to talk about Jesus. He has read the whole New Testament and most of the Old Testament. Unlike any other person I have discipled, when he reads a book of the Bible he shows up at Starbucks with a notepad full of verses and questions from that week's reading.

Mike has dedicated his life to Jesus. He serves when needed. He is working through all the junk life has attached to him over the years, and he is trusting God for everything.

Jesus, thank You for letting me see this.

# Bill

Our first year of planting the church, I got a phone call from a lady who was attending our new church. She said that her adopted daughter needed someone to perform the wedding ceremony for her. I was all for it, but I didn't do weddings without doing premarital counseling.

For the next eight weeks, Becky and Bill showed up at my house for one-hour sessions.

Neither of them had any church background, and their personal beliefs were almost completely opposite of each other's. Becky believed in Jesus but really hadn't dedicated her life to following Him. Bill believed that religion, church, and God was just something you believed in to help you get through life.

Fast forward five years.

After performing their wedding, I hadn't seen or heard from them. It was a Saturday morning, and I got a phone call from Becky. She was crying and could barely speak to me.

"What is wrong, Becky?"

"I caught Bill cheating on me with my best friend. I don't know what to do. Will you talk with Bill?"

I got Bill's number from Becky, and after getting her connected with some help, I called Bill. Before we could even hang up from talking to each other, he was on his way over to my house.

We cried together. We prayed together.

"How can I fix my life?"

"You can't, Bill. Only Jesus can. I know you have always thought it was hog-wash, but Jesus has changed my life, and he can change yours."

I connected Bill with some counseling, and he promised to show up to church the next day.

As soon as the Sunday service was over, I searched for Bill and found him still sitting in the movie theater with his head down and tears rolling down his face.

"How are you doing, Bill?"

"Trinity, when you prayed for me yesterday at your house, I felt something. I have never felt it ever before in my life, but I felt something. When I came in here today and everyone starting singing, I felt the same exact thing."

"For once in your life, Bill, because of the decisions you have made, you are finally realizing that you can't get through life on your own.

You need someone stronger than you and bigger than you. That someone is Jesus. Your heart and spirit are sensitive to feeling it now."

Bill prayed to accept Jesus in his life, and before my eyes and more importantly Becky's, we watched Bill do a 180 in almost every area of his life over the next year.

Bill and Becky are involved in a house church and attend faithfully every Sunday with their three kids. They both were baptized on the same day and have become a symbol of redemption and forgiveness.

Jesus, thank You for letting me see this.

### More and More Fruit

I could go on and on. The names will change and the stories will be somewhat similar for you. Jesus died for people, and that is why we are on mission.

Humanity is God's Plan A. There is no Plan B.

We get to be on the front lines of this grand epic, living out the mission, discipling others, and teaching them to live as Jesus taught us to live.

When this happens—

We will find lives changed. Lives transformed.

The adventure of church planting—with all of its struggles, all of its loneliness, all of its set-backs, all of its failed experiments—has one amazingly sweet fruit: people finding Jesus.

I have been spiritually attacked like no other time during my times as a church planter. I have been depressed and felt like such a failure. When those days come (and they do come), I have always been able to look back at the lives that God has transformed through all of this and realize why we went through what we did. In some ways, this is the least we could do to get the message of God to those who need it.

If this is our cross to bear, then we bear it proudly.

Jesus, thank You for letting US see this.

### My Prayer for You

May the Father of our Lord, Messiah Jesus Christ, bless you beyond anything you could ever contain in your journey to build His kingdom here on earth. May disciples spring forth and multiply over the earth from the community that God has called you to establish. May your city, your country, and your region be transformed through the people who begin to live life like Jesus. I pray that your church community would be blessed a thousand times more than God has ever blessed ours. In the name above all other names, Jesus Christ, we pray this. Amen.

# CHAPTER TWELVE IN REVIEW

*Key Ideas*

1. Church planting is an opportunity for unbelievable spiritual growth.
2. Prayer and fasting take on a new significance when facing a giant-sized challenge.
3. God will work in the lives of people in the community and His plan will be enhanced through their lives and the telling of their stories.
4. It has always been God's plan to work in this world through His followers.
5. God initiated Plan A. There is no Plan B.

*Discussion Questions*

1. What do you expect God to do in your life? How will that affect what He does through your life?
2. How have you experienced spiritual growth during difficult times? What should you expect from a church planting experience?
3. Who are those people through whom God is working? How can you encourage others by telling their stories?
4. Since God's plan involves people, who are the people He is bringing into your ministry? What do you expect Him to do through them?
5. Why are we God's Plan A? What does that say about God's love for us?

*Next Steps*

1. List some things God is doing in your life.
2. Keep a journal of the spiritual victories you experience through this process.
3. Write on a board or the wall the names of the people God is bringing into your community. Make note of their stories.
4. List your vision-driven expectations on the wall. Expand the list as needed.
5. Identify some ways you can engage in building relationships in the marketplace in your community.

# Author Bio

You would think **Trinity Jordan** grew up in a Christian home with a name like that, but he didn't (his father saw two Italian spaghetti westerns—*My name Is Trinity and Trinity Is Still My Name*). He grew up off the Alps in Italy until moving to the United States in 1991, and then moved every year until he graduated from high school. Visiting Christian churches on occasion when friends invited him, he didn't give his life to God until his senior year of high school.

Trinity began his college education at Texas Christian University before transferring to Evangel University, where he received Bachelor of Arts degrees in Biblical Studies and Legal Studies. At the age of nineteen, while in college, he served as senior pastor of a Presbyterian Church. He began working on his Masters in Theological Studies at Assemblies of God Theological Seminary, but he couldn't stand being in school and not ministering full-time, so he and his wife, Ami, left Missouri to be youth pastors at a church in Utah.

Three years later they ventured out to plant Elevation Church (www.elevation.cc) in Layton, Utah. Elevation Church launched a public gathering at a local movie theater in October 2005 with 158 people in attendance, which was a stellar feat for an evangelical Christian church in Utah, and now has multiple house churches, two public gathering locations, 3,800 podcast subscribers, and is working on a third location. Trinity is currently Lead Pastor there and traveling around the country speaking about missional living and church planting.

Trinity works with the Church Multiplication Network as a lead church-planting facilitator, focusing on drawing a younger crowd of leaders. When not preaching at Elevation Church, he speaks at other churches, church-planting events, college campuses, and other events around the world.

Trinity has written the articles "I Am the Church" and "Cool Yesterday, Hated Today" for *Relevant Magazine*. Daniel McNaughton and Trinity co-wrote a discipleship book called *Learning to Follow Jesus*, which is availabe for purchase at www.elevation.cc. He is a blogger at www.trinityjordan.org.